"Remember, the Cap is the most important. It can make or mar your appearance."
— Hector Powe. Naval, Military, R.A.F and Civil Tailors.

British Officers' Peak Caps of the Second World War

Olivier C. Dorrell

Schiffer Publishing Ltd

4880 Lower Valley Road • Atglen, PA 19310

Library of Congress Control Number: 2013956673

Printed in China.
ISBN: 978-0-7643-4578-4

We are interested in hearing from authors with book ideas on related topics.

Published by Schiffer Publishing Ltd.
4880 Lower Valley Road
Atglen, PA 19310
Phone: (610) 593-1777
FAX: (610) 593-2002
E-mail: Info@schifferbooks.com.
Visit our web site at: www.schifferbooks.com
Please write for a free catalog.
This book may be purchased
from the publisher.
Try your bookstore first.

Contents

Dedication

Dedicated to Flight Lieutenant L.B. Lee, Royal Air Force and Pilot Officer Rowan Jackson, Royal New Zealand Air Force. Rest peacefully.

Acknowledgements

I am very grateful to all of the contributors who spared their time in sharing their collections, knowledge, and/or resources. Without them this book could not have been made possible.

Thank you to: The Archive, Gieves & Hawkes Ltd., 1, Savile Row, London W1S 3JR; David Blake AMA, Curator of the Museum of Army Chaplaincy; The Australian War Memorial; The Brown University Library; James Katzenstein, and Mikko Peltoniemi; Stuart Bates, for his knowledge of Victorian Forage caps; George Quigley, for his knowledge of the RCAF; Hans Schleicher; Geoff Newman, of Geoff Newman Militaria; Skipper Greenwade, of www.skippergreenwade.com; Niels Pedersen, of www.militarybadgecollection.com; and Roger Lucy, for not only writing the foreword but for initially having pointed me in the right direction. Lastly but by no means least, I would like to show my sincere gratitude to Tod Rathbone, of the Rathbone Museum of World War II Aviators, www.rathbonemuseum.com, whose collection, both inspirational and enviable, proved vital to this book.

I am especially grateful to Bob Biondi and all the team at Schiffer Publishing. Thank you for all your support and for helping me to realise this project. Not to forget also my family and close friends, for their support and patience, humouring me in my interest.

As a final note, I would like to pay tribute to all those brave men and women, who, in those dark days donned a uniform, and cap, sacrificed so much, and in most cases everything, so that my generation would never have to. May we learn from history and respect the past.

Foreword

It is some two hundred years since the peaked service cap first made its appearance as an item of military uniform. It was first adopted during the Napoleonic Wars as a comfortable piece of campaign dress, in place of more formal and cumbersome shakos, busbies or helmets. In British service, as in other countries, it evolved, over the course of the 19th century into a popular item of officers' undress uniform (that is the uniform worn when not on parade or on other occasions where full dress was required). It reached its full apotheosis in 1902, when as the "Service Dress Cap" it became the universal headgear, for both field and home service of all ranks of the British Army. It was also adopted for wear by officers and petty officers of the Royal Navy and later by the Royal Air Force.

Since the Great War, as other types of head-dress such as the field service cap or the beret have taken over its role as an item worn in the field or for undress, the peaked cap has come full circle to emerge as what is largely a dress uniform item. In doing so it has become much more ornate, and serves as a means to display the wearer's rank, arm of service and "tribal" (i.e. regimental or arm of service) affiliations. The result is a huge range of variations on the original theme in terms of colour, cut, piping, and of course, cap-badges. This variety is made even greater by the degree of license given to military tailors on how exactly these caps should be fashioned. To those worn by the Army should be added the somewhat more standardized caps issued to Royal Navy and RAF. Moreover the armed forces of many Commonwealth countries, which based their uniforms on British patterns, offer their own variety of locally tailored and distinctively badged peaked caps.

Clearly this offers a fertile field to the collector. But any field of collecting is a potential minefield if no proper references exist. There are many books on British uniforms, and also books on British cap-badges. Strangely up to now no one has devoted a book to the British Officer's peaked cap. Olivier Dorrell has now ably stepped into the breach. I am well acquainted with Mr. Dorrell as an informed and passionate collector of combat helmets. He has brought this same passion to this important but neglected subject. A word of warning though, despite its title, this book confines itself neither to Britain, nor to the Second World War. The peaked caps of Commonwealth countries are also discussed, and while the focus of the main body of his book is indeed on the Second World War, Mr. Dorrell very usefully carries his examination of these caps right down to the present day.

Moreover the book begins with an invaluable chapter on the evolution of the peaked cap as an item of military headdress from the early 19th century until the promulgation of the 1904 Dress Regulations for Officers gave the officers' peaked cap its current form. This also provides an opportunity to place the development of the peaked cap in Britain within the context of its evolution on the continent.

Chapters 2 to 6 minutely describe the characteristics of Undress and Service Dress caps of regiments and service of the British Army, with chapters, as well, on the Royal Air Force, the Royal Navy, and related services such as the Merchant Navy and Customs and Excise. Chapter 7 reviews the peaked caps of the major Commonwealth countries: Australia, New Zealand, Canada and South Africa, noting their similarities to and differences from their British counterparts. Chapter 8 describes British officers' peaked caps from 1945 to the present day. These chapters systematically examine, and illustrate, the variations for every section of the cap: the body, the band, the peak, the lining, as well as the badges, piping and braid that distinguishes one unit from another.

The remainder of the book provides a lot of very useful advice to the collector –how to research and determine the date of a peaked cap, spotting frauds, and most important of all – given that we are dealing with cloth artefacts that are now seventy years old – their preservation and proper display and storage. A valuable list of military outfitters known to have supplied peaked caps, and the period within which they operated, is also supplied as well as a price guide. All in all this is a very valuable reference that fills a long-unfilled gap on the collector's shelf. I commend Mr. Dorrell for initiative and diligence in researching and writing this book.

Roger V. Lucy
Ottawa, December, 2012.

Preface

I cannot remember the exact day when my childish interest in old military objects turned into a focused and dedicated collecting hobby. Nor can I explain to a non-collector, what motivates me in this particular field. I could say that it stems from a childhood of watching too many war films, or the desire to preserve historical military artefacts, or even from a need to inform or educate future generations in the social or materialistic aspects of what was used and worn at a certain period.

Of course it is all of these reasons and more, although none of them political. I choose not to collect SS items and my collection remains uniquely military focused. It is a searching and difficult question to answer indeed, regarding why you collect what you collect. I guess I have an appreciation for the artefacts themselves, and of course collecting is an addiction.

As a collector for many years the focus of this book is an area close to my heart. While there is a vast amount of reference books and materials available on Third Reich German militaria, as well as Second World War U.S. equipment, when it comes to British Officer's peak caps of the same period, such information is sadly lacking, which can prove frustrating.

Official documentation in regulations, instructions and patterns does exist, but acquiring this information and deciphering it into one body is no easy feat. While I have strived to provide an in-depth study into the wartime British Army, Royal Air Force and Royal Navy, a certain lack of various aspects, including a complete list of approved Outfitters, prevents me from creating a comprehensive exploration. Perhaps I can address this in a later edition.

Concerning the content itself, I have intentionally repeated certain relevant and key points or features in more than one section of this book, to allow easier referencing and to give a rounded account of a particular topic.

Where certain pieces were unobtainable, I have inserted artist's impressions to provide a representation of a particular piece. Furthermore, the use of illustrations has been included to present a *near real* visual overview of a specific topic. Although accurate in regards to their information, they should not be considered as original wartime pieces, and as such, should not be used in comparison to an actual original, which may vary slightly. These are computer generated images and should be regarded as such.

The main focus of this book concerns the period from 1936 to 1945, although it does provide a brief reference on Commonwealth forces, as well as those used post-war. So whether you are a collector, re-enactor or a curator, this book documents the key features and details that you will need to consider when seeking to identify a British Officer's peak cap to this period, and I hope it can be regarded as a useful handbook in this most important field.

Olivier C. Dorrell
February 2013.

CHAPTER ONE

Introduction & History

The peaked cap, peak cap, Forage cap or visor cap, as it is commonly known, is perhaps the single most identifiable piece of uniform. Employed throughout the world with numerous military forces, law enforcement agencies and civilian organisations, the cap style has become iconic and timeless.

Whether used for Service or Dress the peak cap is elegant and yet commanding, reflecting an evolution that spans nearly two hundred years. It has become one of the most successful forms of military headdress.

With an affinity with the military, why is there a lack of reference material available on this subject? Well the answer is most probably due to several interlinked reasons. The development of a uniform reflects changing attitudes and styles, as well as advances in materials and military roles.

During and prior to the Second World War British Officers' peak caps were supplied by many independent Outfitters and tailored to meet a specific but vague outline given in military regulations. For conformity, Sealed Patterns were kept by the

First World War Royal Navy NCO's cap of W. Paulson ERA4, from 1915. *Private Collection.*

Admiralty, Air Ministry and War Office for uniform accoutrements and insignia. These Sealed Patterns served "to guide make and shape" a cap or item and did not address the material quality, as can be seen from this 1940 dated Sealed Pattern of Field Service cap.

In regard to the actual cap, as well as for the rank device, the Regulations were vague on such details as style and lining, which have the result that many variations of construction and appearance are encountered. Components such as side buttons and chinstraps correspond to a standard specification, along with the design of some army peaks which had to conform to a Regiment's specific requirements. Thus each Outfitter and indeed some caps have their own unique characteristics and identity.

The next question we need to address seeks to answer why Officer's peak caps were of private purchase. Traditionally, in the British military Officers came from the Upper class, which would explain why their uniforms and accoutrements were private purchase, coming from Gentlemen tailors. Officers would join from the University or Public School Officers' Training Corps, and by the start of the Second World War this situation remained unchanged.

History

The evolution of the modern combat helmet can be traced back to the French M1915 Adrian helmet, developed during the First World War. However, the evolution of the peak cap is not so clear. It appears that the military peak cap was of Prussian origin, evolving from the Shako into the Forage cap and through into the style that we now recognise. The name Shako itself derives from the Hungarian csákó süveg, meaning peak cap, which could support this evolution, and certainly the DNA of the Second World War peak caps can be seen in early paintings and illustrations.

The first documented case of the peak cap, as we know it today, can be traced back to the Peninsula War, where it was used by the Prussian Field Marshall Gebhard Leberecht von Blücher and his Officers in 1813 during the battle of Leipzig, and subsequently in the campaign, as is depicted in this 1815 period engraving. This image is also interesting as it provides a comparison to the Shako and suggests this development.

Throughout the 19th Century numerous artworks show the peak cap being worn by Blücher, such as Adolph Von Menzels' "Blüchers Begegnung mit Wellington nach der Schlacht bei Belle-Alliance" or Irish artist Daniel Maclise's mural entitled "The Meeting of Wellington and Blücher," completed in 1861, and situated in the Royal Gallery of the British Houses of Parliament.

The earliest apparent advocates of this type of cap were the Prussian and Russian armies who used this headdress throughout the 19th Century, which is supported by an 1865 portrait of Tsar Alexander II of Russia. Alexander's cap looks startlingly similar to Forage caps used eighty years later.

Interestingly, Germanic student fraternities from the early-1800s used a very similar styled cap to that of the military, a cap style that has changed little over the last two hundred years, and perhaps influenced or even shared its history with that of the peak cap.

The example shown in the photograph dates from around the late-1800s to 1918, considering the appearance of the Bavarian Royal Family's Coat of Arms. The cap is made by Carl Roth of Würzburg which, together with its colour scheme, would suggest a Würzburg fraternity, as can be seen in an 1815 dated watercolour entitled, "Studentisches Stammbuchblatt Würzburg 1815."

The peak is short and made of leather, which has been heavily patented on its topside and textured on its underside. The narrow band is stiffened by leather and features a brown oilcloth style sweatband. The lining is cream coloured silk, with embossed maker's details, while the top is a green felt baize.

However it was in 1825 that the British Royal Navy officially acknowledged the use of a cap to be worn on-board ship. An example of such a cap can be seen in this late Victorian era example of a Royal Navy Officer's peak cap.

Regarding the British Army. Officers used a Forage cap as early as 1835, which can be seen in this elegant watercolour from that time. By the mid 19th Century the cap's shape and details had become more recognisable as is highlighted in this beautiful example from the Light Dragoons.

Landwehr Prussienne. Soldat. Offizier. Pomöranien, c.1815. Engraving: 10.8x11.6cm. Early engraving of Prussian Landwehr, suggesting the origins of the peak cap. Courtesy of the Anne S.K. Brown Military Collection, Brown University Library.

Victorian era Royal Navy Officer's peak cap. The recognisable modern peak cap style was born in the late-1890s. *Private Collection.*

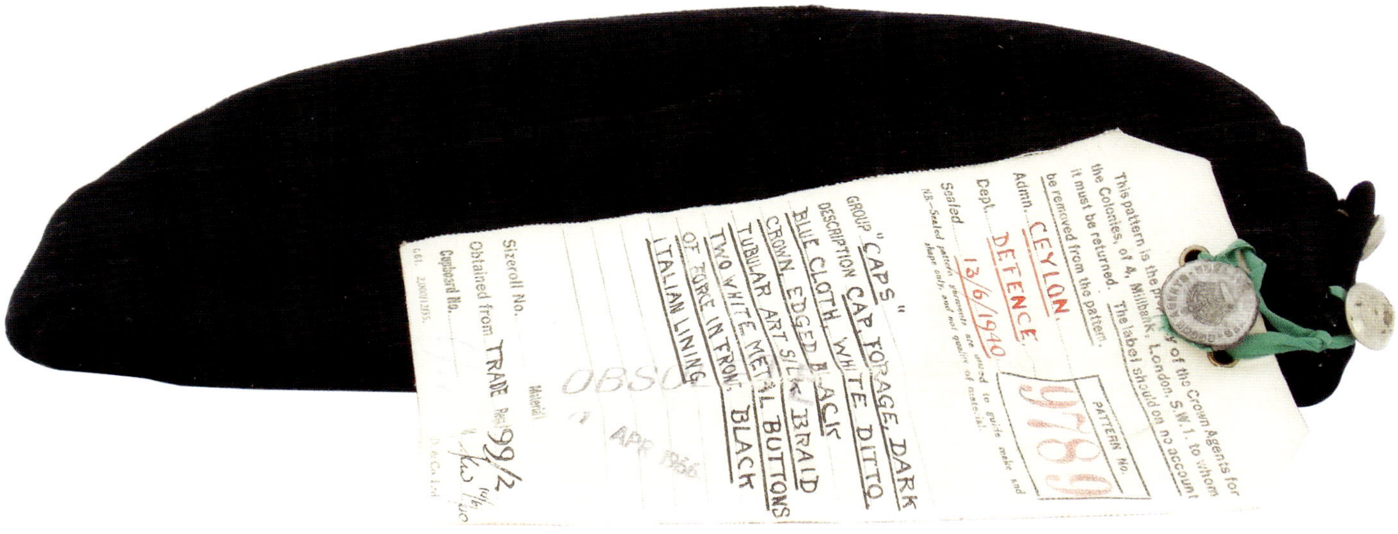

Sealed Pattern FS cap. Note the metal seal with crown. Sealed patterns were used as a master pattern for Outfitters and were kept by the various military ministries. Private Collection.

German student fraternity cap. A style that changed little in its 200-year history. *Private Collection.*

British officer of the 27th Foot, c.1835. Watercolour: 27.9x36.7cm.
An early watercolour study of a British Officer. Note the Forage cap resting on the side table.
Courtesy of the Anne S.K. Brown Military Collection, Brown University Library.

In 1855, with the exception of certain regiments, the Forage cap's peak changed to a more duckbill style, shown nicely on this period example from the 93rd Regiment.

During the latter half of the century the cap took on more of a pillbox form with a peak, resembling a cut down Shako, seen in this South Wales Borderers example from around 1880.

The various styles of Victorian Forage cap can be seen in this 1860 photograph showing Dragoon Officers, where there evidently was an overlap in their use.

By 1879 the Forage cap had become the official headdress for Officer's Morning Dress, and by the end of the 19th Century their form leant towards a distinctive modern appearance. Exhibiting fuller cushioned tops, while their peaks remained short, upright and notably rounded, which is evident in the featured example, which dates from 1900.

This particular cap is probably a Forage cap from an Officer of the 54th Regiment of Foot. The cap body is blue, while the peak is as stated above, with a depth of 4.5cm. Unfortunately, the cap band is missing but would have been black embroidered oak leaf. The chinstrap is black patent leather, measuring 1cm in width with blackened brass hardware, similar to that worn on Royal Navy caps. The side buttons are gilt, hallmarked for Firmin, and are 1.6cm in diameter. The sweatband on this cap is quite narrow at 3.5cm wide, while the lining is quilted, as was the case with most 19th Century Forage caps.

The 1904 Dress Regulations for Officers of the Army gives details on this Forage cap, as well as information on a Service dress cap of the same specification but fashioned to match the material of the service dress jacket.

Forage cap of the 93rd Foot. *Courtesy of the Benny Bough Collection.*

Forage cap of the Light Dragoons, circa pre-1854.
Courtesy of the Collection of Stuart Bates.

Forage cap of the South Wales Borderers.
Courtesy of the Collection of Stuart Bates.

British Dragoon officers, c.1860. Photo: 27.9x35.1cm.
A group photograph nicely showing the various styles of early Forage caps. *Courtesy of the Anne S.K. Brown Military Collection, Brown University Library.*

Late Victorian Forage cap, c.1900. *Private Collection*.

Lining and peak detail of the Victorian Forage cap, c.1900. *Private Collection.*

Studio photograph of a Royal Artillery gunner, dating to 1942. *Courtesy of James Katzenstein.*

Non-Commissioned Officer of the German Army, 1945. Whilst most nations exhibit their own variations in cap style, perhaps the most distinctive examples of this come from North Korea and Russia. *Private Collection.*

Petty Officer of the Royal Naval Reserve, dating to World War I or the early inter-war period. For all peak caps, this inter-war period saw cap tops widened and peaks enlarged. *Private Collection.*

Prior to the early years of the First World War, Army peak caps were worn on active service, however they were soon discovered to offer little protection to the wearer, and with the introduction of Britain's first modern combat helmet in late-1915, they were reserved for non-combat use. Between the end of the First World War and the beginning of the Second World War, the cap underwent minor changes, but in essence remained the same style.

In the modern age there still seems to be a place for the peak cap in Military circles. The Royal Navy, Royal Air Force and British Army still use a No.1 Dress cap and No.2 Service dress cap, although for service wear other forms of headdress, such as the Beret, have taken preference with some Regiments and Units. Across the globe, the peak cap's presence is still strong, with many countries exhibiting their own unique styles.

CHAPTER TWO

Branches

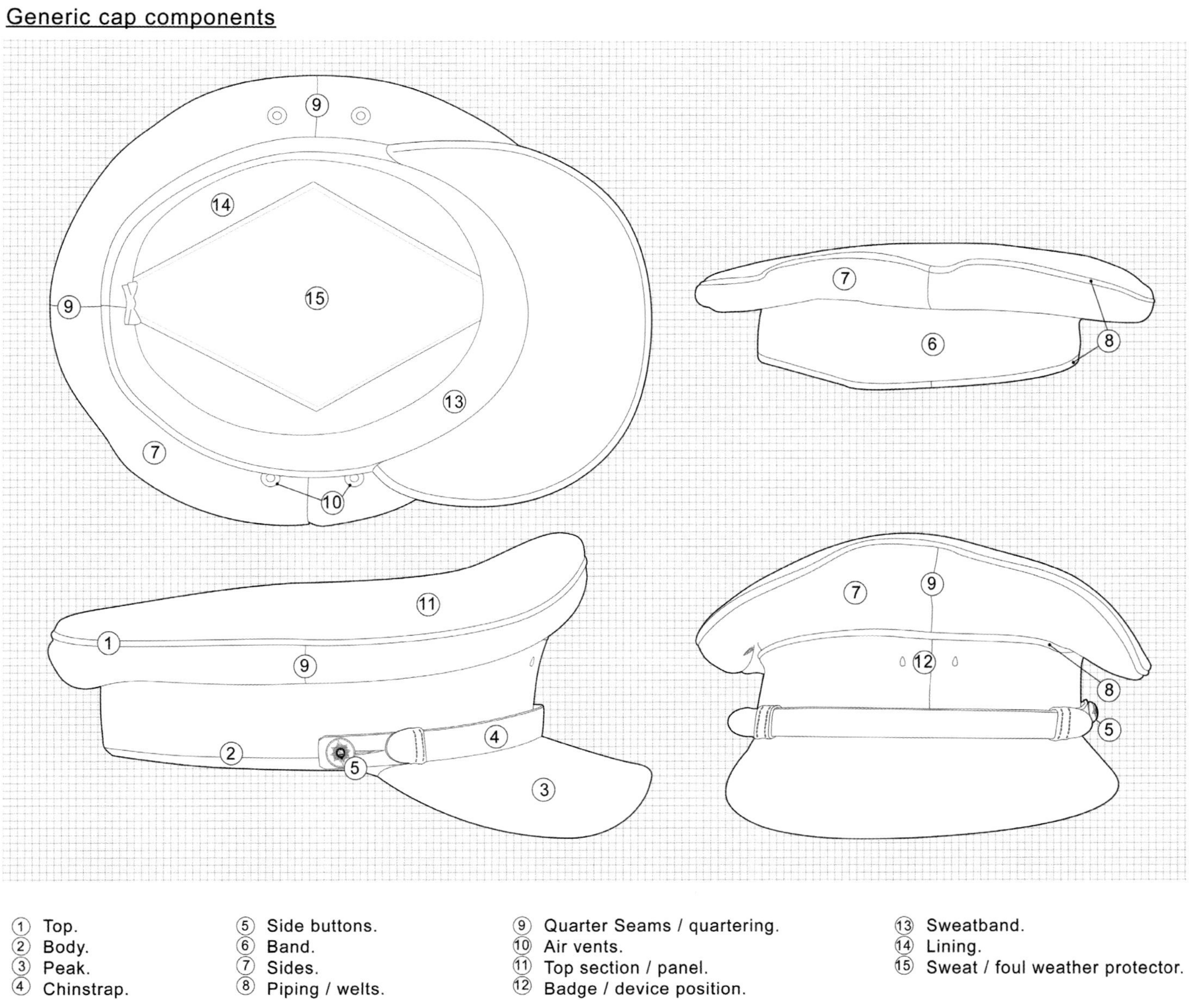

Generic cap components. Illustration.

Although the peak cap was used by all three military branches during the Second World War, not to mention numerous civilian organisations, the overall construction of the cap remained consistent throughout, although cap styles could be as individual as the wearer or the Outfitters, within regulation.

The basic peak cap consisted of a top, body and peak, with the addition of an adjustable leather chinstrap which was fitted over the peak and attached by small side buttons. This was the normal position of wear, although in some situations or occasions the chinstrap was worn as its name suggests.

The top section and band were made from one piece of cloth, and in most cases featured piping running around the top's edging. The material under the top section, known as the Sides, was made up of four pieces of cloth sewn together at the quarter seams. Around the lower edge of the cap was a welt broader than the other piping areas of the cap. Some caps also featured piping at the join between the sides and band. The badge or rank device was fitted at the front of the cap to line up with the frontal quarter seam.

Other than for chinstraps and patent peaks, leather was used to stiffen cloth covered peaks as well as the cap body itself, in certain cases, although this was not usually the case with Army Service caps or those of the Royal Navy. Hardboard and cardboard were employed as stiffeners, as well as weaved Hessian. In the matter of lining, this was left entirely up to the Outfitter.

While the official Dress Regulations issued through His Majesty's Stationary Office used the Imperial measurements, I have made my measurements in centimetres, to aid referencing.

Size comparison of a generic cap side button with that of a tunic. *Private Collection.*

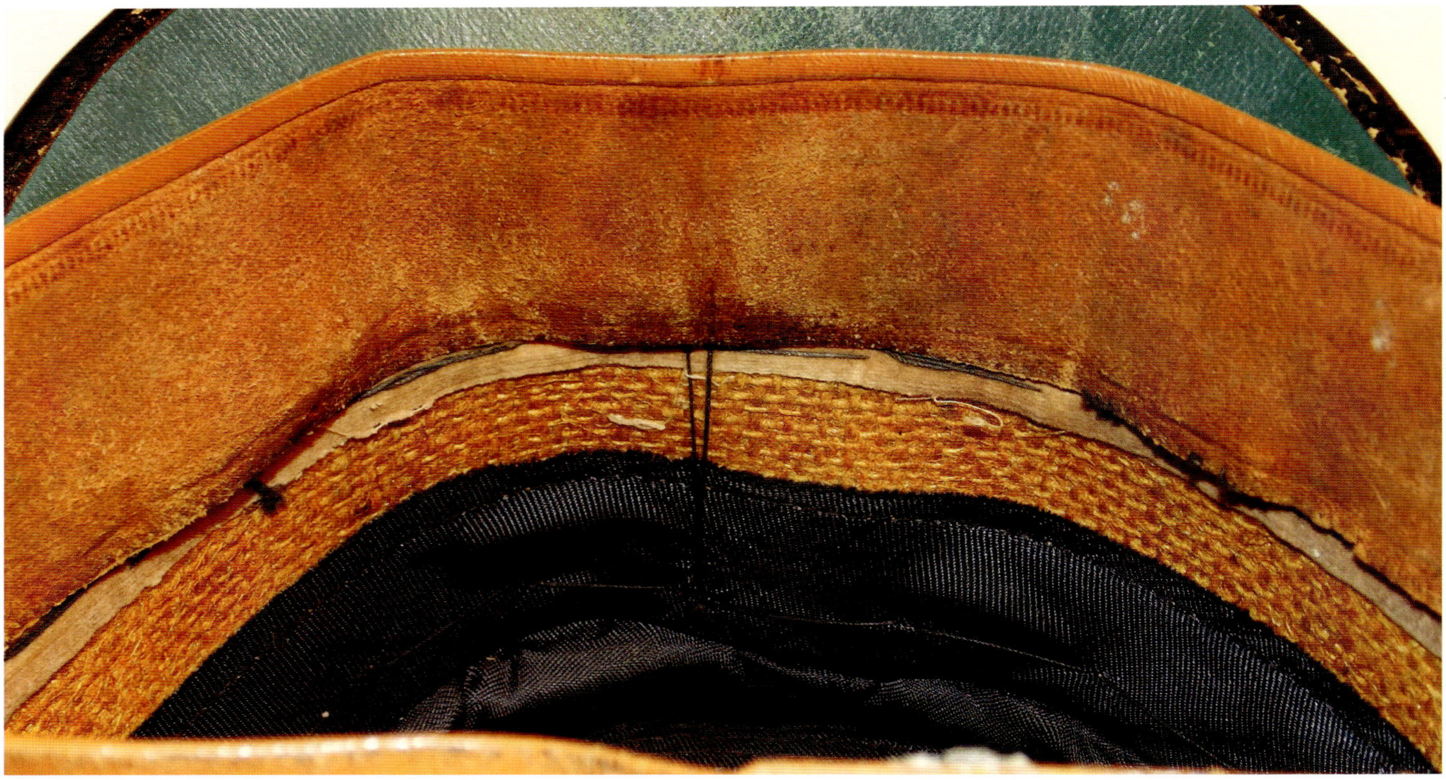

Hessian used as a body stiffener (in this case from a R/N cap). Hardboard, cardboard and leather was also used during the Second World War and previously. *Private Collection.*

CHAPTER THREE

The British Army - Undress

British Army ranks (Undress)

1. Field Marshall.
2. General. Lieutenant-General. Major-General.
3. Brigadier. Substantive Colonel. (Not cadre to Dept. / Corps.).
4. **Field Officers** Lieutenant Colonel. Major.
5. **Junior Officers** Captain. Lieutenant. 2nd Lieutenant.

British Army rank chart illustration (Undress).

During and prior to the Second World War the Forage cap and Service cap were the mainstay of the British Army, however, we must take into consideration the fact that certain regiments, maintaining regimental history and customs wore their tradition forms of headdress.

Other than the Scots Guards, Scottish Regiments wore the Glengarry cap for undress and the Tam o'Shanter for service dress, while the Royal Tank Regiment wore the black beret with flash for undress and the black beret without the flash for service dress. British Army Full Dress uniforms often consisted of a helmet as headdress.

The last official Dress Regulations for the Army, prior to the Second World War, was the 1934 edition, amended in 1938. Although the Regulations give a specification that was used by both forms of the peak cap, it fails to mention certain in depth details of material, size and style.

Brass cap badge support, covered in the lining material. This particular example hinges at the middle. *Private Collection.*

Rank Structure of the British Army:

General Officers:

Field Marshall
General
Lt-General
Major-General

Colonel
Brigadier

Field Officers:

Lt. Colonel
Major

Junior Officers:

Captain
Lieutenant
2nd Lieutenant

Undress - Junior Officers

Officially termed as the *Cap, Forage, Universal Pattern*, the Dress cap was similar in construction to that of the Service cap, but was designated strictly for formal and ceremonial occasions. Only Senior Officers and those of the Foot Guards and Household Cavalry were authorised to wear their Forage cap with their Service dress uniform.

Cap Body

The top and body of the Forage cap was constructed from dark blue/ black felt. Leather or hessian was most commonly used as the body stiffener, measuring 4.4cm wide. The width of the body was 3.8cm. Brass plates were used to support the area behind the cap badge, although a crown stiffener was not inserted. Coloured piping ran around the top edging, which denoted a particular Regiment or Corps.

The Sides of the top were 5.4cm in width and constructed from four separate panels which were not padded. Blackened brass or metal air vents were situated each side of the side quarter seams. Post-war Undress or Dress caps do not seem to have the addition of the air vents.

Some regiments however used different cloth colours to distinguish themselves apart, which are detailed below:

Infantry:	**Colour:**
Light Infantry.	Green.
Rifle Regiments.	Rifle green.

Corps/Department:	**Colour:**
Corps Of Military Police.	Scarlet.
The Royal Army Chaplains Department.	Black.
Lieutenants of London/Counties.	Dark blue.
Military Knights of Windsor.	Blue.

Cavalry:	**Colour:**
Dragoon Guards.	Blue.
5th Royal Inniskilling Dragoon Guards.	Dark green.
Hussars (excluding below).	Waterloo red.
11th Hussars.	Crimson.
13th/18th Hussars.	White.
15th/19th Hussars.	Scarlet.
Lancers.	Blue.
12th Lancers.	Scarlet.
16th/5th Lancers.	Scarlet.

In addition to or alternatively, different piping colours were used:

Infantry:	**Colour:**
Infantry of the line.	Scarlet.
The Royal Fusiliers.	Scarlet.
The Royal Inniskilling Fusiliers.	Scarlet.
The Royal Irish Fusiliers.	Scarlet.
The Royal Welsh Fusiliers.	Scarlet.
The King's Regiments.	Scarlet.

Infantry

General Officer. (Staff).

Brigadier/Substantive Colonel. (Staff)

Line Infantry. (Field rank).

Line Infantry. (Worcestershire Regiment).

Royal Fusiliers.

The Rifle Brigade. (Field rank).

The Rifle Brigade.

Coldstream Guards.

Grenadier Guards.

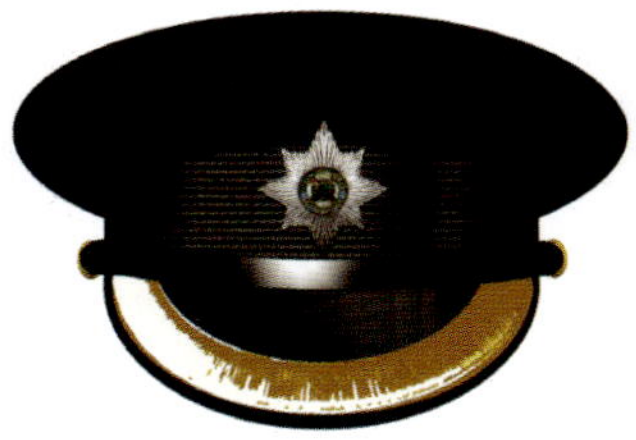
Irish Guards.

Scots Guards.

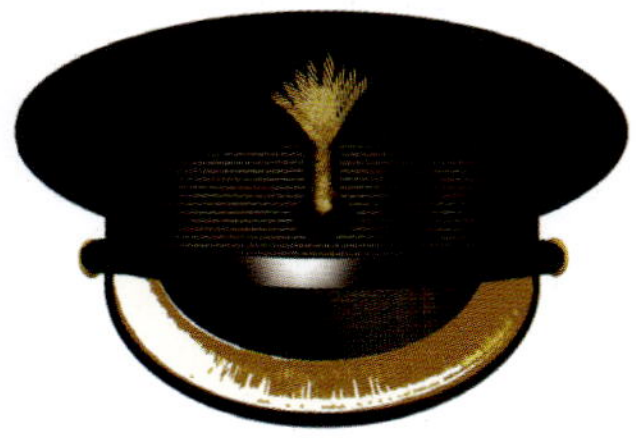
Welsh Guards.

Support

Royal Artillery.

Royal Engineers.

Royal Engineer Services. Staff. (Major and above).

Royal Corps of Signals.

Corps./Department

Lieutenant of County. (England).

Military Knights of Windsor.

Royal Military Academy Sandhurst.

Royal Military College.

Colour distinction chart for Infantry, Support and Corps/Department Forage caps. This can be used for identification purposes but keep in mind that colours may vary slightly with these illustrations.

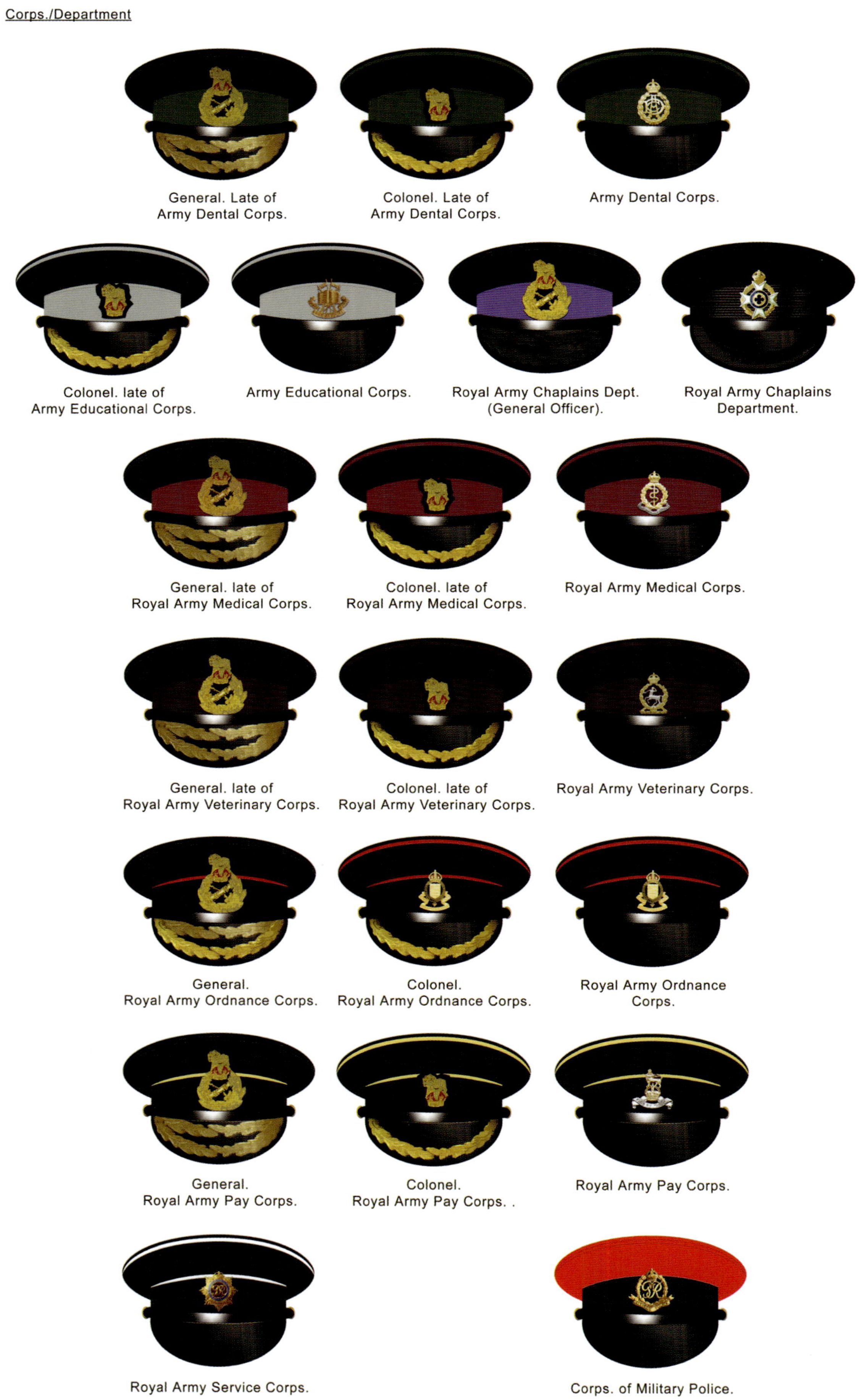

Additional colour distinction chart for Corps/Department Forage caps.

Cavalry

Colour distinction chart for Forage caps of the Cavalry.

Some regiments however used different cloth colours to distinguish themselves apart, which are detailed below:

Infantry:	**Colour:**
Light Infantry.	Green.
Rifle Regiments.	Rifle green.

Corps/Department:	**Colour:**
Corps Of Military Police.	Scarlet.
The Royal Army Chaplains Department.	Black.
Lieutenants of London/Counties.	Dark blue.
Military Knights of Windsor.	Blue.

Cavalry:	**Colour:**
Dragoon Guards.	Blue.
5th Royal Inniskilling Dragoon Guards.	Dark green.
Hussars (excluding below).	Waterloo red.
11th Hussars.	Crimson.
13th/18th Hussars.	White.
15th/19th Hussars.	Scarlet.
Lancers.	Blue.
12th Lancers.	Scarlet.
16th/5th Lancers.	Scarlet.

In addition to or alternatively, different piping colours were used:

Infantry:	**Colour:**
Infantry of the line.	Scarlet.
The Royal Fusiliers.	Scarlet.
The Royal Inniskilling Fusiliers.	Scarlet.
The Royal Irish Fusiliers.	Scarlet.
The Royal Welsh Fusiliers.	Scarlet.
The King's Regiments.	Scarlet.
Light Infantry.	Green.
Royal Regiments.	Scarlet.
The King's Royal Rifles.	Black.
The Rifle Brigade.	Black.
The Royal Ulster Rifles.	Black.
Coldstream Guards.	As cap.
Grenadier Guards.	As cap.
Irish Guards.	As cap.
Scots Guards.	As cap (Gold around top).
Welsh Guards.	As cap.

Corps/Department:	**Colour:**
Corps Of Military Police.	Blue (Scarlet around top).
The Army Dental Corps.	Emerald green.

Field Officer's cap of the Royal Engineers, circa pre-1936. *Private Collection.*

A rare example of a mid-war Royal Army Chaplain's Department Forage cap, 4th Class, for the rank of Captain. Note the black piping detail and black woven band. The outfitter is Alkit Ltd. *Private Collection*

The Army Educational Corps	Cambridge blue.
The Royal Army Chaplains Department.	Black.
The Royal Army Medical Corps	Dull cherry.
The Royal Army Ordnance Corps	Scarlet.
The Royal Army Service Corps	White.
The Royal Army Veterinary Corps	Maroon.
The Royal Army Pay Corps	Primrose yellow.
Military College (Cadets).	Scarlet.
Lieutenants of London/Counties.	Scarlet.
Military Knights of Windsor.	Blue (Scarlet around top).

Support:	**Colour:**
Royal Artillery.	Scarlet.
Royal Horse Artillery.	Scarlet.
Royal Electrical and Mechanical Engineers.	Scarlet.
Royal Engineers.	Scarlet (also around the top of the band).
Staff of Royal Engineers Services.	Bright blue.
Royal Corps of Signals.	As cap.

Cavalry:	**Colour:**
Dragoon Guards.	As on respective facings.
1st The Royal Dragoons.	Scarlet.
3rd Carabiniers.	Yellow.
4th/7th Royal Dragoon Guards.	Royal blue.
5th Royal Inniskilling Dragoon Guards.	Primrose.
The Queen's Bays.	Scarlet.
The Royal Scots Greys.	Blue.
Life Guards.	Scarlet.
Royal Horse Guards.	Scarlet.
11th Hussars.	Crimson.
13th/18th Hussars.	White (blue on the body).
15th/19th Hussars.	Scarlet.
Lancers.	As on respective facings.
12th Lancers.	Scarlet (blue on ¼ seam).
16th/5th Lancers.	Blue.

(Lancers have piping down quarter seam).

Undress cap showing the stipulated 45° peak angle. *Private Collection.*

Field Officer's cap of the Worcestershire Regiment. *Private Collection.*

For ranks of Lt. Colonel and Major that were extra-regimental or not party to a Corps or Department:

> **Cloth colour:** Dark blue.
> **Piping colour(s):** Scarlet and as the cap on the top.

For ranks below that of Major, extra-regimental or not party to a Corps or Department:

> **Cloth colour:** Dark blue.
> **Piping colour(s):** Scarlet and scarlet on the band.

Peak Variations

The topside of the peak and rim consisted of black patent leather, whilst the underside tended to be green skiver leather, with a maximum width of 4.4cm. Cardboard was used to give the peak stiffness. From plan view the peak took the form of a "C" in shape and was angled at 45 degrees.

Regimental Field Officers holding the rank Lt. Colonel or lower wore a wide gold embroidered braid band mounted onto the peak's topside, 1.9cm wide. The addition of this feature caused the peak to be 5cm, at its widest point. Worth noting is that Regimental Officers of the Household Cavalry and Guards also wore the gold braid band, regardless of the Field rank distinction.

The exceptions to this were the Foot Guards and Household Cavalry which used a shorter and more upright peak, with a band of gold embroidered braid. Field Officers of the Rifle Regiments also wore a single row of blackened oak-leaf mounted onto the peak topside.

The peak detail on Army Chaplains, holding the rank of Major and Lt. Colonel, had a blackened braid band mounted onto the topside,

Field Officer peak detail: Moss Bros.

Field Officer peak detail: Alkit.

Field Officer's peak variations. Note the "C" shape. *Private Collection.*

A typical example of a badge used on the Forage cap. *Private Collection.*

The gilt and silver cap badge worn by Army Chaplains. Observe the wreath detailing. This design of badge was worn by ranks below Substantive Colonel, inclusive. Badges worn by Jewish Chaplains substituted the Maltese cross with the Star of David. Note that Service cap versions were blackened metal. *Private Collection.*

measuring the same as that of Field Officers, as specified in 1938 Dress regulations. It would appear that during the Second World War this detail changed to gold-wire, and remains as such with current issue Forage caps. Certainly, the Deputy Chaplain-General's cap, featured later in this chapter, serves to support a pre-1953 date change.

Cap Badge

The cap badge is similar to that worn on the Service cap and was either embroidered, silver and gilt or gilt.

Band

The band was fitted around the body of the cap and sewn into position. It was coloured and patterned according to the specific Regiment or branch. Officially the band measured 3.8cm wide, although width varied slightly. For example, the black oak-leaf band on this KC Worcestershire Regiment cap measures 4.2cm in width.

Infantry:	**Colour:**
Infantry of the line.	Black oak-leaf lace.
Fusiliers.	Scarlet felt.
King's Regiments.	Scarlet felt.
Light Infantry.	Black oak-leaf lace.
Royal Regiments.	Scarlet felt.
The King's Royal Rifles.	Black mohair.
The Rifle Brigade.	Black mohair.
The Royal Ulster Rifles.	Black lace with shamrock pattern.

Oak-leaf band detail, showing sewn seam. *Private Collection.*

Coldstream Guards.	Black mohair.
Grenadier Guards.	Black mohair.
Irish Guards.	Black mohair.
Scots Guards.	Regimental check.
Welsh Guards.	Black mohair.

Corps/Department:	**Colour:**
Corps Of Military Police.	Blue felt.
The Army Dental Corps	Emerald green felt.
The Army Educational Corps	Cambridge blue.
The Royal Army Chaplains Department.	Black mohair.
The Royal Army Medical Corps	Dull cherry felt.
The Royal Army Ordnance Corps	As cap.
The Royal Army Service Corps	As cap.
The Royal Army Veterinary Corps	Maroon felt.
The Royal Army Pay Corps	As cap.
Military College (Cadets).	Scarlet felt.
Lieutenants of London/Counties.	Scarlet felt.
Military Knights of Windsor.	Scarlet felt.

Support:	**Colour:**
Royal Artillery.	Scarlet felt.
Royal Horse Artillery.	Scarlet felt.
Royal Engineers. As cap.	
Royal Electrical and Mechanical Engineers.	Scarlet felt.
Staff of Royal Engineers Services.	Bright blue felt.
Royal Corps of Signals.	Black oak-leaf lace.

Cavalry:	**Colour:**
Dragoon Guards.	As on respective facings.
1st The Royal Dragoons.	Scarlet felt.
3rd Carabiniers.	Yellow felt.
4th/7th Royal Dragoon Guards.	Royal blue velvet.
5th Royal Inniskilling Dragoon Guards.	Primrose felt.
The Queen's Bays.	Scarlet felt.
The Royal Scots Greys.	White vandyked.
Life Guards.	Scarlet felt.
Royal Horse Guards.	Scarlet felt.
11th Hussars.	Crimson felt.
13th/18th Hussars.	Blue felt.
15th/19th Hussars.	Scarlet felt.
Lancers.	As on respective facings.
12th Lancers.	Scarlet felt.
16th/5th Lancers.	Blue felt.

Ranks below that of Major, not cadre to a particular Regiment, Corps or Department, wore a scarlet band with a blue inner central stripe, 2.8cm wide.

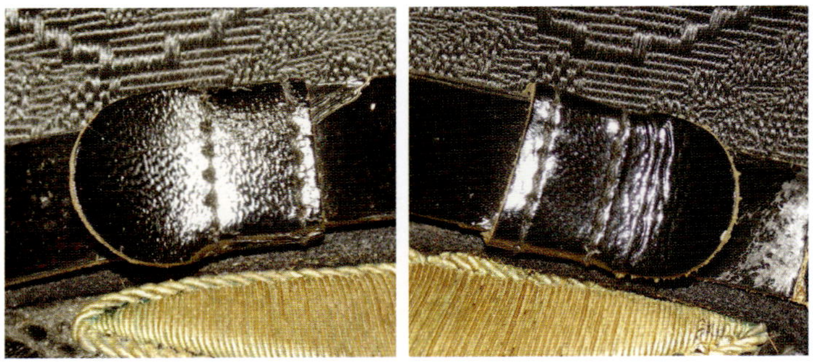

Crescent slide chinstrap detailing from a wartime Forage cap. Note the orange peel surface texture to the patent leather. *Private Collection.*

Diamond slide chinstrap detailing from an early Forage cap. Like the crescent variation, the pattern and style could vary. *Private Collection.*

Covers

Whilst outside the United Kingdom and in conjunction with the White Mess dress, ranks of substantive Colonel and higher were authorised to wear their Forage cap with a white cover. For occasions when the Service dress uniform was used, a khaki top cover was also permitted.

Chinstrap

Aside from the Scots Guards who did not wear any chinstrap, all Forage caps featured a black patent leather chinstrap similar to that used on Royal Air Force Officer's peak caps. Pre- and early-war chinstraps had a width of 0.9cm, while later examples were wider, at 1.2cm, a difference that can be observed on the two examples of Colonel's Forage caps.

Chinstrap dimensions:
Length 48cm (varies).
Width 0.9cm.

Leather faced slides were used to adjust the chinstrap length or for decoration. These were sewn onto the chinstrap and were either crescent shaped or that of a half diamond.

Half crescent slide dimensions (pre-1953 cap):
Length 2.2cm.
Height 1.5cm.

Side Buttons

The side buttons were gilt and of the same pattern and dimensions as those worn on the Service cap. They were to be positioned at the end of the peak. Again, for Forage caps belonging to the Scots Guards, no side buttons were present.

Cap lining example showing a full top oilskin sweat protector. *Private Collection.*

Cap lining example showing a full top celluloid sweat protector. *Private Collection.*

An example of a Royal Army Chaplain's Department gilt Forage cap side button, worn by ranks of Major and lower. The design reflects that of the cap badge, albeit for the crown position. The side button worn on the Service cap was of a similar pattern but in blackened metal. *Private Collection.*

Overview of a gilt side button, unmarked. Circa pre-1953. *Private Collection.*

Substantive Colonel/Brigadier's Forage cap, not cadre to regiment or corps. Note the diamond chinstrap slides. Circa World War I or early inter-war period. *Private Collection.*

A rare Brigadier's Forage cap, of the Royal Army Chaplain's Department. Worn by Deputy Chaplain-Generals. This cap dates from mid/late war and was used beyond 1953, from its QC added side buttons. Forage caps for Substantive Colonel wore the gilt and silver cap badge, in place of the Royal crest. *Private Collection.*

Dimensions:

Diameter	1.5cm.
Depth	0.6cm

Lining

The lining was similar in construction to that of the Service cap, although the material colour was usually darker, in some cases violet, with an oilskin or celluloid sweat protector covering the entire top section. Sweatbands also tended to be a darker coloured leather and were around 5cm in width.

Undress - Senior Officers

The dress cap for Senior Officers is identical in dimension and construction to that of Junior Officers, other than in regard to rank distinction and piping. Worth noting is that the majority of these peak caps seem to have been supplied by either Herbert Johnson or Hawkes & Co. Ltd.

Cap Body

The cap was constructed from dark blue woollen felt with coloured piping around the crown edging. For the ranks of Field Marshall and General Officers* the cap details are as stated:

Cloth colour: Dark blue.
Piping colour(s): Scarlet. As cap on top.

For ranks of Brigadier and full Colonel (Extra-regimental, not party to a particular Corps or Department):

Cloth colour: Dark blue.
Piping colour(s): Scarlet. As cap on top.

An illustrated impression of a wartime General Officer's Forage cap. A khaki cover would have been worn over the top for Service dress.

Army and Navy "scrambled eggs" comparision.

Note the difference in style of the oak-leaf peak detailing. Royal Navy examples resemble a more obvious oak leaf profile, being notable rounded. *Private Collection.*

Substantive Colonel / Brigadier cap badges.

Variations in size and style of Colonel and Brigadier cap badges, used prior to 1953. *Private Collection.*

A KC General Officer's cap badge. *Private Collection.*

*General Officers, Brigadier and Substantive Colonels, previous to a certain corps, wore the coloured piping and felt band of that particular corps. (Refer to the piping colours mentioned in the Junior officers section for reference).
For Army Chaplains with the rank of Substantive Colonel and higher:

Cloth colour: Black.
Piping colour: Purple.

Peak Variations

The peak detail used by Colonel and Brigadier, was black patent leather with a dark green skiver underside. A single row of gold oak-leaf adorned the topside. Ranks of Lt. Colonel and Major, not cadre to a Regiment of Corps wore the peak of a Field Officer.

Grades of General, and the rank of Field Marshall, were distinguished by a double row of oak-leaf mounted to the topside. As with Junior Officers, Senior Officer's peaks have an obvious "C" shape in plan view. It should also be noted that the oak-leaf style used by the Army and Royal Air Force differs in style somewhat from that used by the Royal Navy.

Senior ranking Chaplains used the same oak-leaf rank distinction, mounted to the peak topside, as their regular army counterparts, although the oak-leaf was black in colour. This black detailing was later changed to gold-wire. While the changeover date is unclear, it appears to have been after 1938, most probably mid-wartime, as can be observed in the Deputy Chaplain-General's Forage cap example.

Cap Badge

The rank device for Colonel and Brigadier, consisted of the Royal Crest: a lion surmounting the crown. The badge was fully embroidered with gold-wire bullion, coloured thread, and plush red felt for the crown lining. The backing, which was black felt, was sewn onto the felt band. Dimensions varied. However, it must be noted that a Colonel of the Royal Army Ordnance Corps wore the same cap badge as junior RAOC Officers, although by the 1970s the Royal Crest was also used.

Device dimensions (Pre/early example):
Height (exc. Backing) 4.3cm.
Width (exc. Backing) 3cm.

Device dimensions (wartime example):
Height (exc. Backing) 4.9cm.
Width (exc. Backing) 4cm.

Ranks of General and Field Marshall used a similar construction to the embroidered Colonel's badge. In the case of General Officers, the device consisted of a crossed baton and sabre over a black

George V's Lt. Colonel, Substantive Colonel and Brigadier's gilt side button. Wartime examples substituted the V for a VI. *Private Collection.*

Senior Officer's Forage cap lining. This example is typical of early caps and those of the inter-war period. Note the pale sweatband and drawstring. Also note the interesting velvet softener at the lower edge of the forehead area. *Private Collection.*

Senior Officer's Forage cap lining, wartime. In contrast to the early example that is reminiscent of a cloth helmet lining system, the overall lining style and sweatband of this example is characteristic to the vast majority of wartime Forage caps. *Private Collection.*

felt background, surrounded by a laurel wreath and surmounted by the Royal crest. The blade of the sabre was silver. The device was affixed directly to the felt band, and usually had a pale paper backing. While dimensions varied slightly they tend to have a height of 6.5cm with a width of 5cm, as is the case with the highlighted example.

Note the maker's label displaying the original price of 16 shillings and sixpence. At the time of writing, the price for such a badge, in this condition, would be around £70 Sterling. Expect to pay higher for a better example.

For Field Marshall the device was identical in style and dimensions to that of the General Officers, save for the difference of two red trimmed crossed batons instead of the baton and sabre configuration. The badge backing was paper.

The Royal Army Chaplains' Department (RAChD): For Christian Officers, the cap badge worn by the Chaplain-General and General Officers was as that worn by their regular counterparts, whilst the Royal Crest was worn by Deputy Chaplain-Generals.

Chaplains holding the rank of Colonel and lower wore a silver Maltese cross positioned in front of a gilt laurel wreath, surmounted by a crown. The cross detail consisted of a centrally mounted circular blue plate underneath of a gilt quatrefoil and frame. For Jewish Chaplains, the style of the badge was similar although the Maltese Cross was replaced by the Star of David.

Band

The felt band was usually sewn onto the cap body and measures 3.8cm wide. As with the piping, General Officers, Brigadiers and substantive Colonels wore the coloured piping of their previous corps. Regarding Field Marshall and ranks of General Officers, the cap band was scarlet in colour. This was also the case for Brigadiers and full Colonels, not cadre to a particular Regiment, Corps or Department, as well as Staff Officers.

For Lt. Colonels and Majors, not cadre to a particular Regiment, Corps or Department, the band was scarlet with a blue centre, 2.8cm wide. Chaplains with the rank of Lt. Colonel and higher wore a purple coloured cap band.

Chinstrap

The chinstrap was black patent leather and was the same as that used by Junior Officers.

Side Buttons

Side buttons used on Senior Officer's peak caps reflected those used on their Service cap, being gilt with specific rank motif and measuring 1.27cm in diameter. The Royal Cypher detail, used on Lt. Colonel, Substantive Colonel and Brigadier's side buttons, as well as Staff Officers, was marked G *VI* R, for the period of 1936-1953, whilst caps dating from the reign of King George V, 1910-1936, were marked G *VI* R, as pictured.

Lining

Senior Officer cap lining was of a similar configuration to the Service peak cap but of a notable higher grade, while a clear celluloid sweat protector usually covered the entire top section.

CHAPTER FOUR

The British Army

Service Dress – Junior Officers

The Cap, Service Dress, as it was designated for Junior Officers, was of the universal Pattern and was constructed to match the material used on the Service dress uniform.

Cap Body

The body, top and peak were made from brown wool barathea, or in some cases a finer woollen felt. Piping was situated around the top edging whilst the Sides were made up of four separate pieces of cloth, which were sometimes padded around the cap badge position. Some early war examples also have piping situated around the top edge of the band.

Dual air vents were located on the sides above and astride of the button positions, or each side of the rear seam, and were painted brown or khaki brass. The air-vents measured around 0.7cm or 0.9cm in diameter, and either has a riveted rear side or split-pins.

A period photograph of a Royal Army Service Corps Captain. *Private Collection.*

A rare and unique example of a Royal Fusiliers Service cap. Note the double row of stitching around the top in place of crown piping, more reminiscent of an RAF cap. Perhaps not surprising as the maker is Bates Hatter. *Private Collection.*

British Army ranks (Service dress)

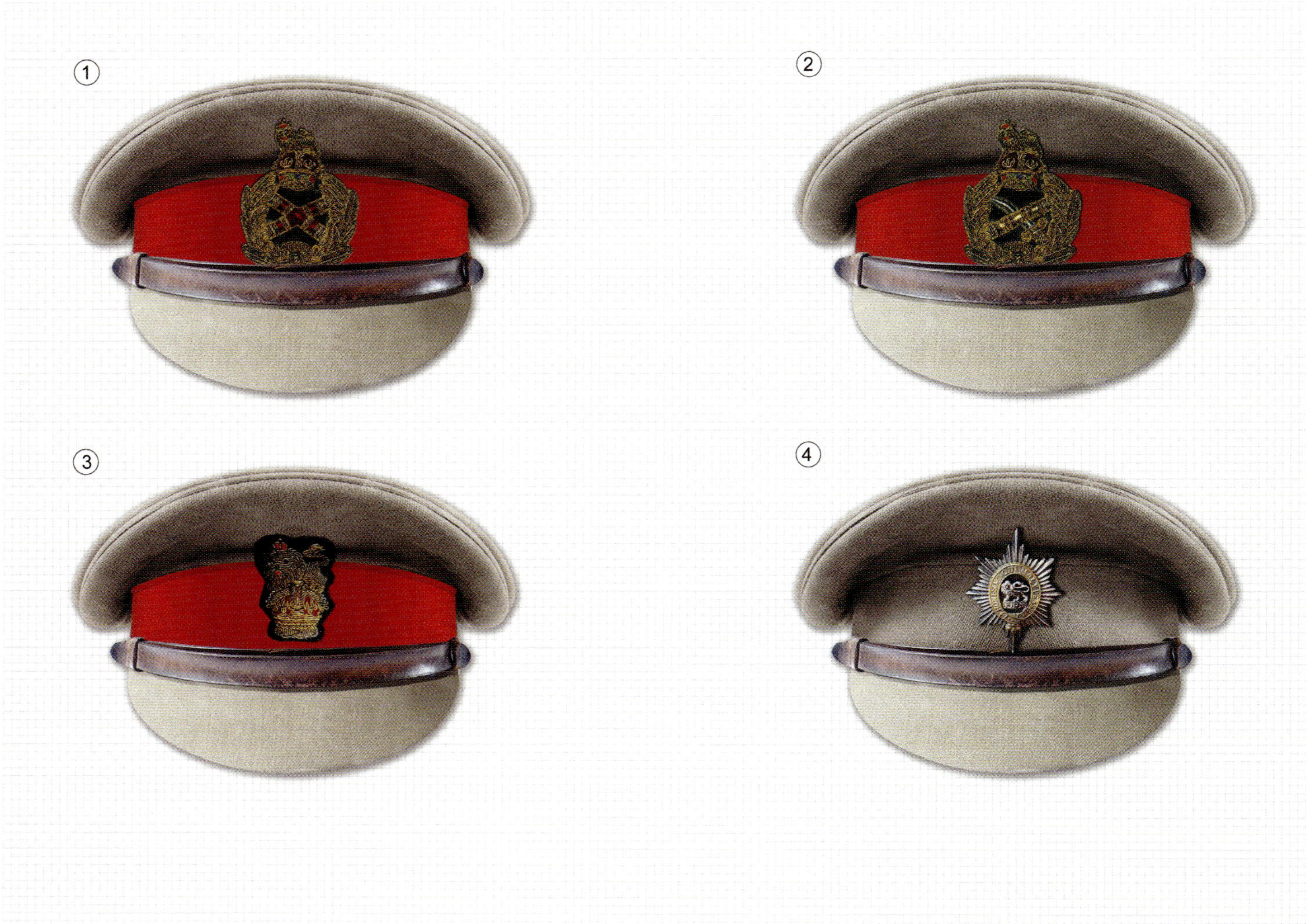

(1) Field Marshall.

(2) General.
Lieutenant-General.
Major-General.

(3) Brigadier.
Substantive Colonel.

(4) Major.
Captain.
Lieutenant.
2nd Lieutenant.

British Army rank chart illustration (Service).

Typical air-vents used on Service caps, seen here positioned at the rear. *Private Collection.*

Air-vents from the Bates cap, lacking the addition of metal eyelets. This uncommon feature can also be seen on the wartime Bates RAF Group Captain's cap in Chapter 5. *Private Collection.*

Service cap air-vent backing detail: riveted and split-pins.

Air-vent backing attachment, showing rivets and split-pins. *Private Collection.*

The *Stiff* pattern Service cap. *Private Collection.*

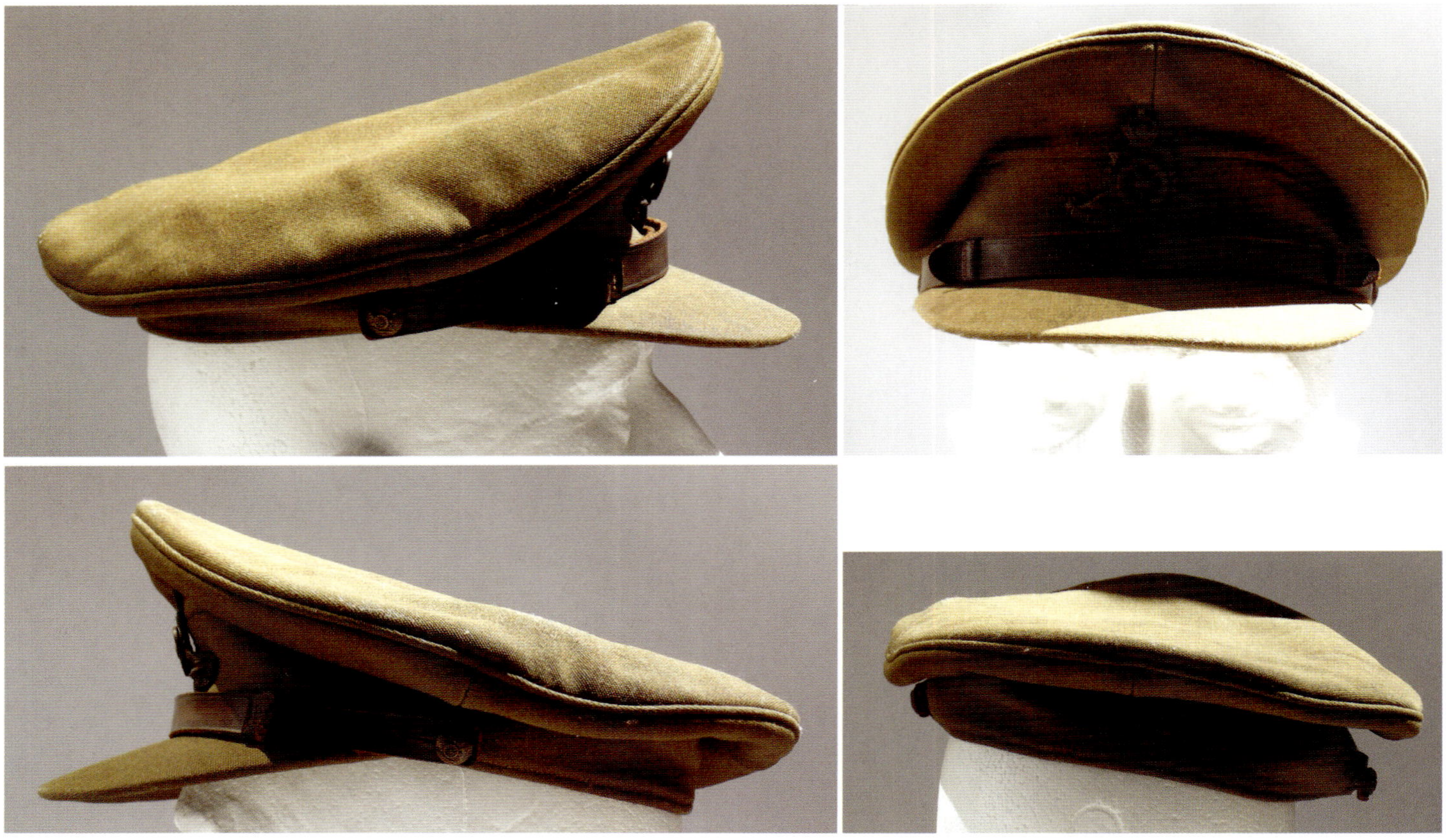

An pictorial overview of a typical *Soft* pattern Royal Artillery Service cap. *Private Collection.*

An early war Service cap of the Scots Guards, missing its badge. Note the two attachment holes. *Private Collection.*

The service cap came in two patterns, *Stiff* and *Soft*.

The *Stiff* pattern had the addition of a wire stiffener around the top lining, creating a disc style appearance, similar to those of the First World War, and used a leather band stiffener.

The *Soft* pattern had a durable peak and was not usually fitted with a crown stiffener. The band also tended to use a hessian weaved stiffener, which was quite flexible, as well as a similar stiffener or brass stiffener for behind the badge area.

Peak

Inter-war and wartime peaks had a distinctive wide "D" shape, where both their topside and underside were cloth covered khaki, fitting with the rest of the cap. In some rarer cases peak undersides were greened leather. Hardboard, cardboard or leather was used to provide peak stiffness.

Cap Badge

Entire books have been written on British cap badges, so I merely wish to touch upon the essentials that are relevant. Peak cap badge size varied according to regiment while the materials also varied. Badges were either made from bronze, silver, gilt or bi-metal, which varied in colour and finish. For Army Chaplains below the rank of Substantive Colonel, a blackened metal badge was used.

The badge was secured to the cap through two slits in the body, positioned directly at the front of the band, and was attached using either split-pins that bent inwards after insertion, or using the lug & pin system. According to regulations of 1943, the cap badge was to be positioned facing forward on the cap and mounted in the middle of the band.

With metal becoming a precious commodity, so called economy badges made of Bakelite plastic were introduced in 1941. By mid-1942 all new badges were plastic, unless construction proved physically possible. The badge finish and colours were

A typical "D" shaped army peak. *Private Collection.*

A rare Service cap of the Worcestershire Regiment fitted with a Sterling silver cap badge. Note the width of the chinstrap compared to that of the Scots Guards cap, which would signify it as a mid-war period cap. *Private Collection.*

made to match that of the metal badges, and can be found in variations of brown, silver, yellow or black. Attachment was with brass split-pins. Plastic badges can warp over a period of time, and thus may also exhibit stress cracks.

Chinstrap

A brown leather chinstrap was worn over the peak and attached using the side buttons. The only exceptions to this were the Rifle regiments and the Royal Army Chaplains Department, which used a black patent leather chinstrap in place of the brown.

Chinstrap dimensions:

Length	48cm (varies).
Width	0.9cm.
Side button slit	2cm or 2.5cm.

Regulations specified the chinstrap width to be 0.9cm, however many wartime army caps had a wider chinstrap, at either 1.2cm or 1.5cm. Interesting to note also is a 1939 period Royal Army Pay Corps Service cap example displays a chinstrap with a width of 1.6cm.

The length of the chinstrap could be changed using the leather slides, which either had a half crescent or diamond shaped wing piece. The dimensions of the slides varied from the different makers but conform to an overall dimension.

Half crescent slide dimensions (mid-war caps):

Length 2.1cm.
Height 1.8cm.
(Chinstrap width 1.5cm).

Cap badge detail with the pin & loop attachment. *Private Collection.*

The pin & loop attachment compared to the slide variation. *Private Collection.*

Split-pin attachment from a Royal Artillery cap badge example. *Private Collection.*

The Bakelite cap badge, used from 1944, was introduced as a temporary measure in response to the wartime material shortages. The badge backing was maker stamped and featured the split-pin attachment method. This particular example is from the Royal Army Ordnance Corps. *Private Collection.*

Components of the Service cap chinstrap. Note the similar configuration to that of the Forage cap. *Private Collection.*

Half diamond slide dimensions (pre/early war):
Length 2.1cm.
Height 1.3cm.
(Chinstrap width 0.9cm).

Slide detail also varied. Examples exist with vertical seams running down the slide's face, which could also encompass the entire slide.

Side Buttons

The side buttons were a half dome in shape and made from bronze. They either displayed the badge of the regiment or corps, or the General List emblem. General list side buttons were used by Officers and men who had not yet been assigned a specific posting, and it was often the case that the buttons remained unchanged even after the fact, which is why this feature is most commonly encountered.

Side buttons were positioned just after the corners of the peak and were half-oval or convex, when seen in side profile. Army Chaplains used black buttons, as were those used by Rifle regiments which were made of Blackhorn.

A Gieves Ltd. Royal Army Pay Corps Service cap, made from high quality thick felt. The chinstrap is purely for appearance and cannot be adjusted. Notice also its width that is uncharacteristically wide for its date of 1939, no doubt the Officer or Outfitter wished to add a little extra flare. *Private Collection.*

Close-up details of the crescent chinstrap slide adjuster. Note the sewn seams. *Private Collection*

Crescent slide from a Royal Artillery cap, note also the sewn seam detail. *Private Collection*

Example of a diamond slide adjuster. Like the crescent slide this style could also vary slightly, as can been seen on the Royal Marine Service cap. *Private Collection.*

Dependent on the Outfitter, buttons could be maker marked and were either polished bronze or browned bronze, and were sewn onto the cap body using thread, through a protruding metal loop. Presumable Bakelite plastic buttons were introduced at the same period as Bakelite cap badges, in 1941, but are seldom encountered on peak caps.

Side buttons dimensions:

Diameter	1.3cm.
Width	0.5cm – 0.7cm.

The featured illustration chart should be used to identify a button to a particular regiment, corps or department. Please bear in mind that it is not designed to be a guide to originality or dating.

A General List cap button. *Private Collection.*

A Blackhorn Rifle Brigade cap button. The side button for Army Chaplains was also black. *Private Collection.*

Lining

Lining style, material and quality differed, even with examples coming from the same Outfitters, although a leather sweatband was a constant feature to all peak caps. It should be noted however that those sweatbands blind embossed with "Real Roan Leather" do not identify a cap to wartime, as Herbert Johnson used such sweatbands on their post-1950s peak caps.

Sweatband dimensions:
Height 5cm/5.3cm.

Sweatband were stitched around the inner body edging and peak, joining at the back. The join was usually stitched closed with a small ribbon mounted at the top of the seam. Often a piece of medical tape was stuck on the backside to re-enforce the join. The leather surface was either textured or left plain, and usually had an embossed rim.

A bronze cap button from the Royal Fusiliers. *Private Collection.*

The lining material was silk twill, cloth or green baize, and was usually covered by a sweat protector, although not in all cases. The lining top section was sometimes padded and could also be flat or quilted in various patterns. It tends to be a gold silver in colour.

Sweat protectors could encompass the entire top section of the lining or merely a diamond shaped area, similar to those of German World War II peak cap linings. Some Outfitters also used the diamond protector as a maker's label. Transparent celluloid protectors were used by the higher end Outfitters, and covered the whole top. These are quite rigid but tend to crease and have a rattling sound when moved.

Most sweat protectors however, used a brown semi transparent oilskin which either took the form of a diamond or covered the entire top. From age and storage they become quite sticky and

A browned bronze cap button from the Royal Army Pay Corps. *Private Collection.*

A blind embossed Real Roan Leather sweatband marking, found on wartime and post-war peak caps. Note also the patterned texture of the leather surface. *Private Collection.*

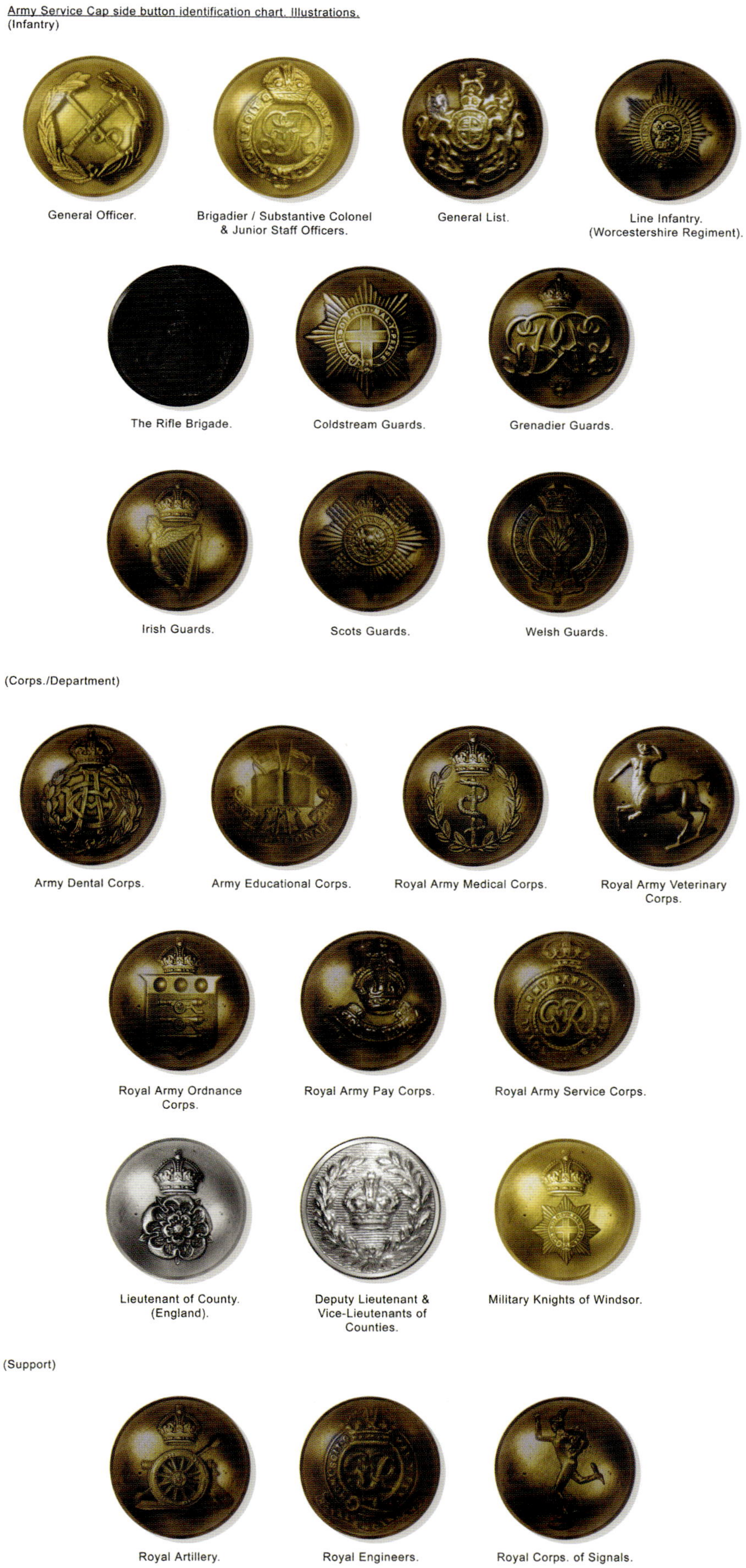

A quick identification chart for Army Service cap side buttons. The most commonly encountered tend to be those of the General List or Royal Artillery.

On some peak caps a strip of medical tape was used to re-enforce the rear side of the sweatband's sewn seam. *Private Collection.*

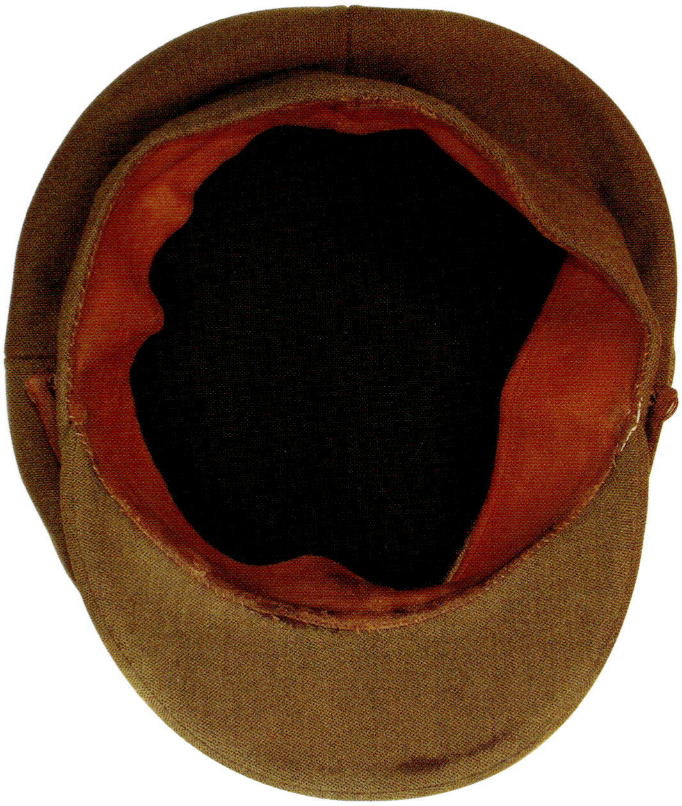

Green baize lining, typical of a Bates or Thomas & Stone cap lining. *Private Collection.*

An example of a padded lining with a diamond maker's label found on this Service cap. *Private Collection.*

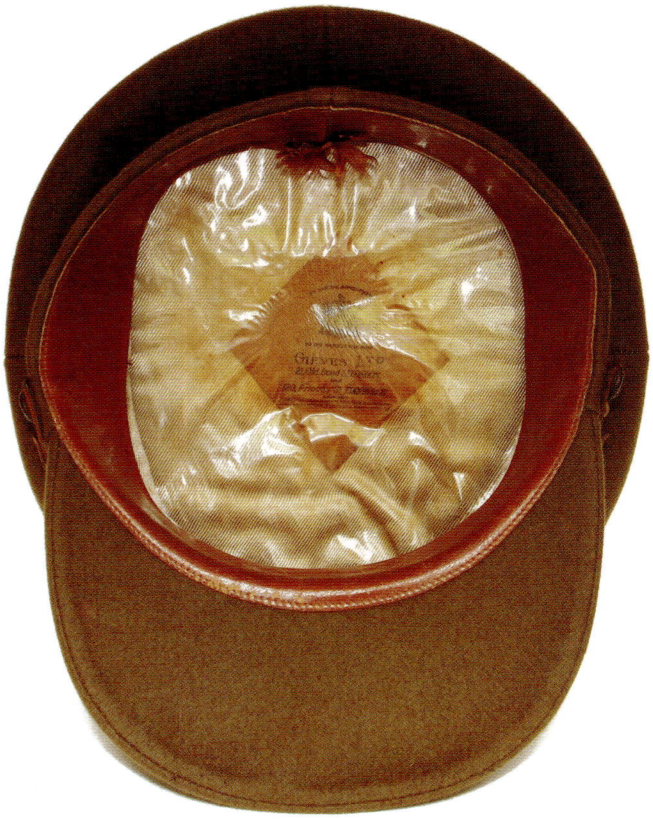

A celluloid sweat-protector used on this prestigious outfitter's Service cap. Note the ribbon at the top of the sweatband's seam. *Private Collection.*

tend to shrink into themselves, exposing the cap lining underneath. While they are not brittle, this effect allows them to be torn or ripped easily.

Service Dress – Senior Officers

Senior Officer's service caps were similar to the *Cap, Service Dress* of the Junior Officers however a difference can be noted in the quality and material, as well as from the prestigious makers label.

In the Dress Regulations they were officially designated the *Cap, Khaki, Service Dress* and were to be worn on manoeuvres, training and active duty. Senior Officers of the ADC, AEC, RAOC, RAMC, RAPC, RAVC, and the Royal Army Chaplain's Department wore their Forage cap with a khaki cover.

Cap Body

The cap body and top was usually made from brown wool barathea, with body coloured piping around the top edge. In some cases a higher grade felt was used. Overall, these caps can display either of the style patterns, although the *soft* style seems to have taken preference in the latter war years.

Peak Variations

Unlike the Dress cap, the Service cap displayed no distinction of rank on its peak. The peak was covered in the same cloth as the cap body and top, and in most cases both the topside and undersides are cloth covered, although some examples are known to have the dark greened leather undersides.

Cap Badge

The rank device consisted of the same embroidered gold-wire bullion badge used on the *Cap, Forage, Universal Pattern.*

Band

A red felt band was worn around the cap body to denote Officers of Field Marshall, General Officers and Staff Officers. Note that the bands from other branches of the British Army were coloured specifically to denote their distinction, such as a band of dull cherry for the Royal Army Medical Corps, or in the case of the Royal Pay Corps, a band of dark blue with primrose piping at the top edge was used.

Chinstrap

The chinstrap is as that used on the *Cap, Service Dress.*

Side Buttons

Side buttons were of the same configuration as those of the Junior Officers, with the exception of being gilt. Specific distinction was displayed for Field Marshall and General Officers, as well as for and Brigadier and Colonels, as used on their Forage caps. It is also worth mentioning that Service caps used by DL's can display black side buttons.

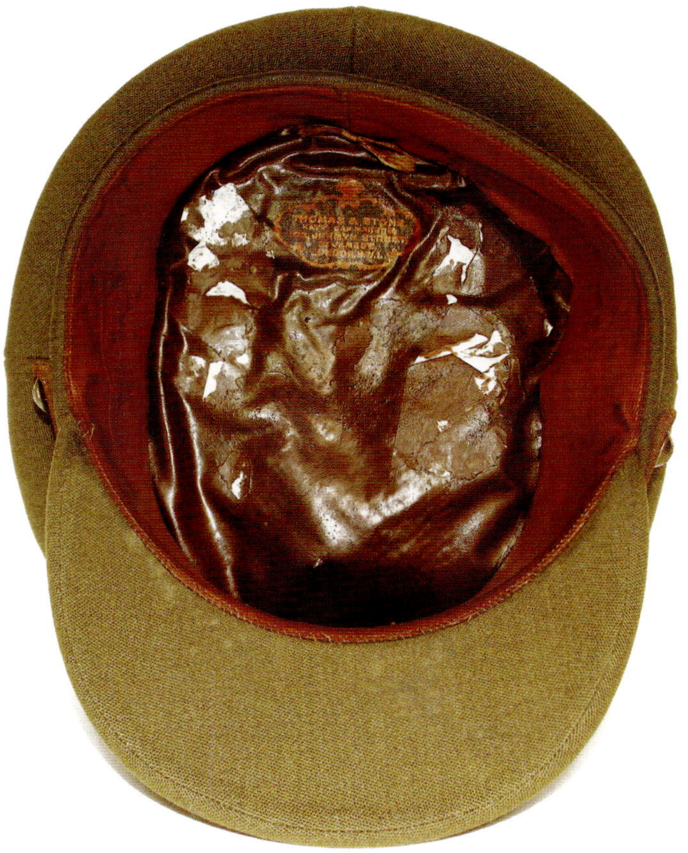

An undamaged full top oilskin sweat protector. The lining material on this particular cap is green baize. *Private Collection.*

A typical Service cap lining. Note how the oilskin sweat protector has ripped, revealing a large section of the lining cloth below, as well as the maker's label. *Private Collection.*

A General Officer's Service cap, showing the correct gilt side buttons and red band. *Courtesy of Tod Rathbone. Rathbone Museum of World War II Aviators.*

A beautiful example of a Royal Army Pay Corps Colonel or Brigadier's Service cap. The cap band is blue and topped by primrose yellow piping. *Courtesy of James Katzenstein.*

Lining

The lining used in senior Officer's Service caps differed little from that of the Junior Officers, however in some cases a finer quality material and finish was used, depending on the maker and the Officer's requirements or position. Note the full top sweat protector in the highlighted General Officer's cap example.

A close-up view of a gilt General Officer's side button. *Courtesy of Tod Rathbone. Rathbone Museum of World War II Aviators.*

The Local Defence Volunteers and Home Guard

Formed in May 1940, the Local Defence Volunteers was created to help defend against the imminent Nazi invasion of the British Isles, after France capitulated. Renamed the Home Guard in July 1940, volunteers could serve for the duration of the war, and comprised mainly of boys too young to serve or men of retirement age, as well as those in reserved occupations.

The initial uniform was civilian clothing with the addition of an armband attached to the right sleeve, but as the pressure on resupplying the evacuated British Expeditionary Force eased, Officers and men were equipped with a similar uniform to the army, all be it of a lower quality.

The Field Service Cap, badged up to the regiment of the county, served as the standard headdress throughout the Home Guard ranks, which is documented in this example from a Lieutenant of the 4th Worcestershire Regiment Home Guard that operated around the Evesham area of Worcestershire (WOR).

The badge used on the Service Dress cap was that used by the men; however ranks of substantive Colonel and above wore a gilt Royal Crest badge, in place of the local regiment. Construction and style was the same as the regular army and so distinguishing a cap to the Home Guard is near impossible, unless it has provenance or is researchable. As such the details in the *Service Dress - Junior Officers* section is relevant.

However a unique exception was the peak cap used by the Upper Thames Patrol unit of the Home Guard. The cap colour, style and construction was similar to that of the Royal Navy *Blue cap*, while the cap badge consisted of a brass Thames Conservancy device, with the abbreviation of UTP, mounted into a black cloth shield with gold-wire edging. A wartime photograph of such a cap can be seen on page 265 of Brian L. Davis' excellent book, *British Army Uniforms & Insignia of World War Two*.

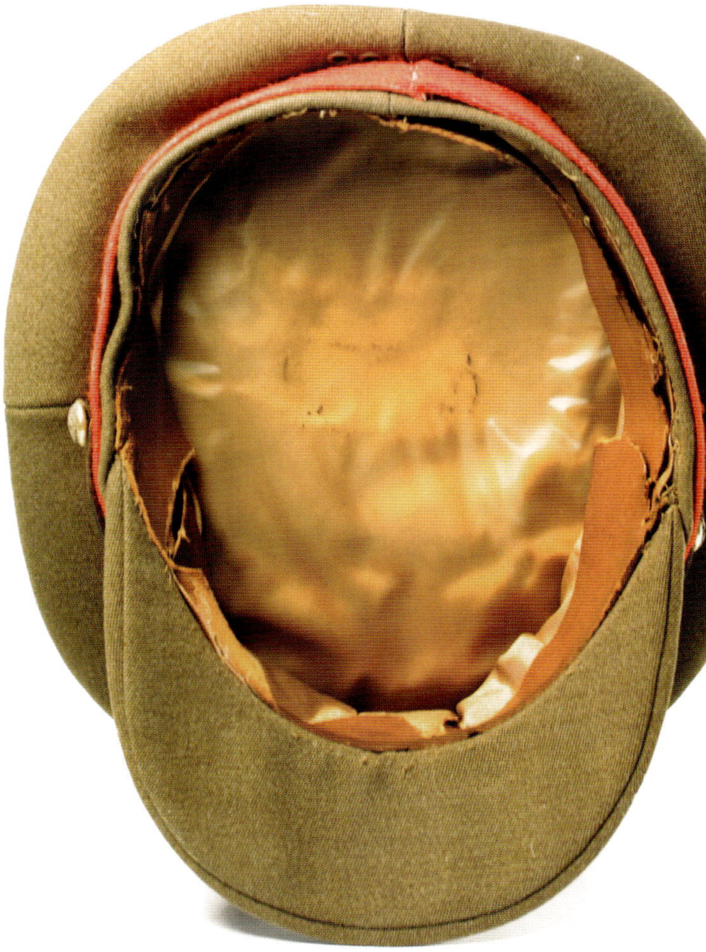

Lining from a General Officer's Service cap. Note how on this example, the red band is not sewn to the cap body. *Courtesy of Tod Rathbone. Rathbone Museum of World War II Aviators.*

Military Knights of Windsor

An institution originally dating back to the 1300s, the Military Knights of Windsor are a collection of retired Officers, with a similar status to that of the Chelsea pensioners. Their duties are mainly ceremonial, serving Windsor Castle.

During the period of 1936-1945, the Forage cap used by the Military Knights of Windsor was of the universal pattern. The badge comprised of a gold embroidered shield showing a velvet St. George cross, whilst the side buttons were gilt, displaying the garter star surmounted by the Imperial Crown. Refer to the Forage cap colour illustration charts.

A typical Field Service cap used by Lt. H.J. Cotton D.C.M. of the Home Guard. As opposed to popular myth most Officers, like their men used the FS cap as opposed to a peak cap. *Private Collection.*

A rare example of a Home Guard's peak cap unique to the Upper Thames Patrol. Note the chinstrap and flat cloth covered side buttons, are those used by the R/N. *Private Collection.*

Lieutenants of the City of London & Lieutenants of Counties

The Lieutenant of the City of London, or of Counties, acted as the official representation for the reigning Monarch in their absence. Often a retired Officer, the Lieutenants main duties were ceremonial or as a Royal escort, for a specific region.

Peak caps used by Lieutenants were nearly identical in construction and appearance to army Forage caps. The cap top and crown piping was dark blue whilst the band was scarlet. The chinstrap was black patent leather with slide detailing, and attached by white metal side buttons. The button detail reflected that of the badge, or in the case of Deputy and Vice-Lieutenants, it displayed the Imperial crown surrounded by a laurel wreath. The cap lining was as that used on high-ranking officer's Undress caps.

As with General Officers, grades of Lieutenant were also distinguished by peak detail. Consistent to all caps however, was a black patent leather topside and rim with a green skiver underside. Lieutenants of the City of London, Deputy Lieutenants and Vice-Lieutenants wore a single row silver oak-leaf mounted to the peak topside, whilst Lieutenants of Counties wore a double row of silver oak-leaf.

The cap badge was made from gold embroidery and was surmounted by the Monarch's crown. For Lieutenants of Counties the badge icon was specific to that particular national region. For England this consisted of a Tudor rose, for Scotland the thistle, for Wales the three ostrich plumes, and for Ireland the Shamrock. The Deputy Lieutenant's cap badge does not feature the crown. For Lieutenants of the City of London, the icon consisted of a gold embroidered City emblem.

Lining from the Upper Thames Patrol peak cap. Again in the Royal Navy style. *Private Collection.*

A pre-1920s Deputy Lieutenant's Forage cap, possibly dating from the First World War period. Lieutenants and Deputy Lieutenants acted as the official representation for the reigning Monarch in their absence. *Private Collection.*

A King's crown Deputy Lieutenant's side button, made from white metal with bronze backing and loop. Unmarked. *Private Collection.*

The embroidered gold wire Tudor rose cap badge, denoting an English Deputy Lieutenant. *Courtesy of Tod Rathbone. Rathbone Museum of World War II Aviators.*

A beautiful example of a post-1953 Deputy Lieutenant's peak cap. As can be observed on the World War I period cap, the specific design did not change over the course of the 20th Century. *Courtesy of Tod Rathbone. Rathbone Museum of World War II Aviators.*

CHAPTER FIVE

The Royal Air Force

Peak caps were used by all ranks of the Royal Air Force, although those used by Warrant Officers and Airman were of a notably inferior quality. Furthermore, unlike in the Army, the RAF used a standard design of peak cap for both service and dress.

A period photograph of a Royal Air Force Flight Lieutenant. *Private Collection.*

Rank Structure of the Royal Air Force

Marshal of the Royal Air Force.
Air Chief Marshal
Air Marshal
Air Vice Marshal
Air Commodore

Group Captain
Wing Commander
Squadron Leader
Flight Lieutenant
Flying Officer
Pilot Officer

Warrant Officer (Non-commissioned officer rank)

Officially designated as the *Cap, Service Dress,* the quality was dependent to its use and/or the limitations of an Officer's purse. Leather flight helmets were used for piloting or crewing an aircraft on a mission, whilst the service cap was reserved for ground-based duties or when travelling in a passenger capacity. Examining period photographs serves to support this.

Cap Body

The top and body of the Service cap was made from blue grey barathea wool. A band of hessian or leather provided stiffness to the body, whilst cloth or hessian was used to support the area behind the badge, as well as removable or non-removable crown stiffeners. This was not the case however with every period cap, where no crown stiffeners were used.

Early cap examples used a double row of white stitching around the top edging, while later wartime caps used piping. Senior Officer caps tended to use the latter. The Sides of the top were constructed from four cloth panels which were entirely padded, or just padded behind the device area. Blackened metal or brass air vents were positioned each side of the Side quarter seams, and measured 0.9cm.

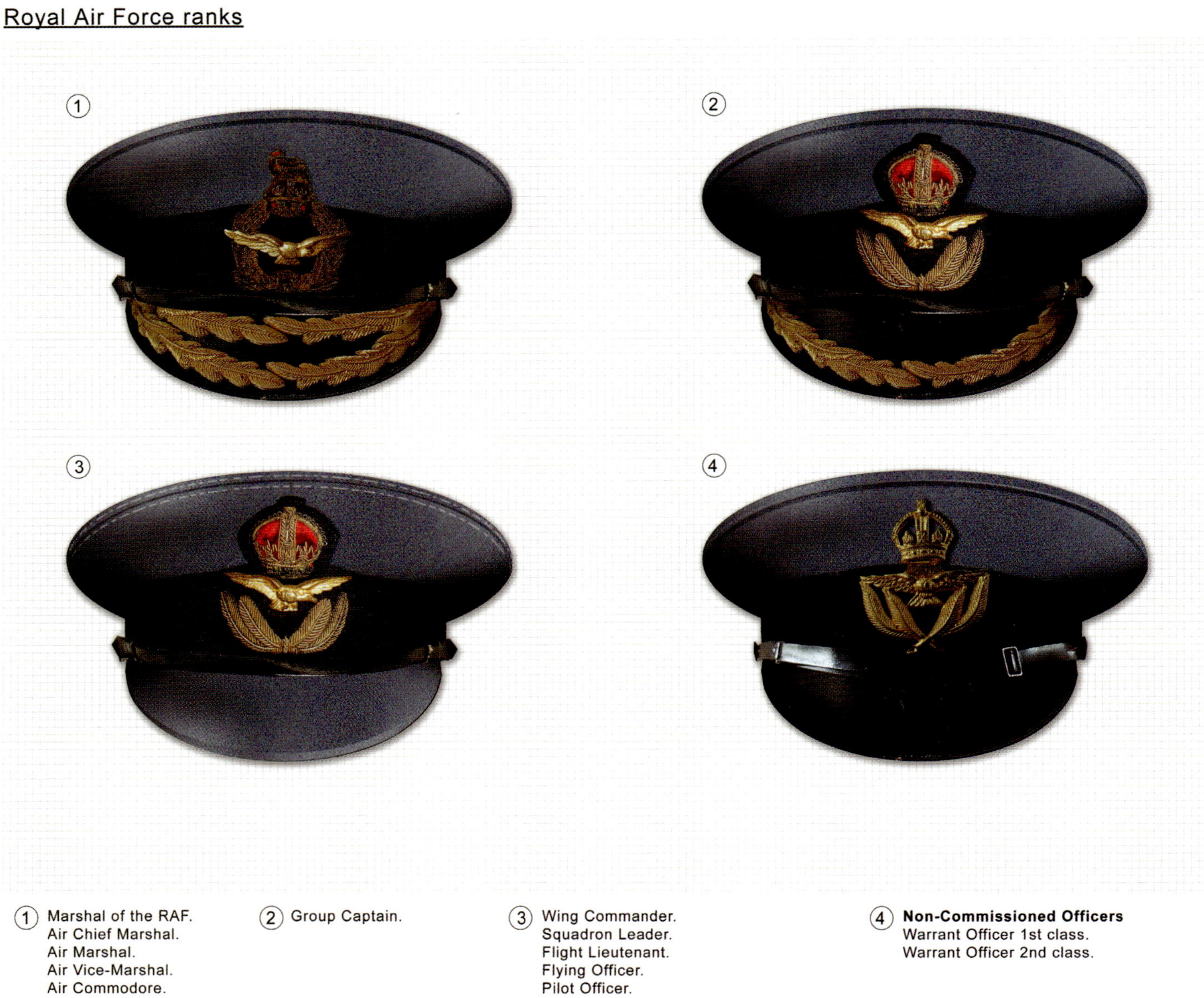

Royal Air Force rank chart illustration.

A close-up view of the hessian band stiffener used on most officer's caps, as well as those of Non-commissioned Officers, as is highlighted in this photograph.
Private Collection.

A late wartime cap attributed to a Flying Officer Serota, dating to 1945. Note the width of the chinstrap. *Private Collection.*

This Austin Reed peak cap is part of a uniform grouping and dates to 1942. Attributed to Flight Lieutenant L.B. Lee, who with his crew were tragically killed in action in 1943, whilst on an anti-submarine mission. Note the narrow chinstrap width. *Private Collection.*

A wartime cap attributed to Pilot Officer Weir of the ATC (Air Training Corps). Again the width of the chinstrap would indicate this as being an early war cap. *Private Collection.*

Peak Variations

A characteristic of Second World War RAF caps is the "D" shape to the peak, seen on all Officer ranks. The peak was specified to be 5.7cm at its widest point and angled to 45 degrees, in comparison to the cap body. The peak was stiffened either by leather or a type of hardboard material.

Junior Ranks

Peak cap material used the same barathea cloth as the cap body, where examples exist with either a fully clothed peak or with a green skiver leather underside. The former group of peak caps are more abundant. It is widely believed that the greened peak underside signifies an early wartime or inter-war cap, a fact that is disputed by some collectors.

When you consider the number of Outfitters that supplied the Royal Air Force, the possibility of both variations existing simultaneously, as with Army peak caps, is plausible. In my personal opinion however, the use of skiver on Junior RAF Officer's caps would suggest an earlier cap date, especially when featured in conjunction with a narrow width chinstrap.

Painted black brass air-vents typical of those worn on all Royal Air Force peak caps. *Private Collection.*

A Royal Air Force Officer's peak cap made by Gieves Ltd. Whilst not uncommon, this Outfitter mostly outfitted R/N Officers.
Courtesy of Tod Rathbone. Rathbone Museum of World War II Aviators.

The two variations of peak style used on Junior Officer's caps. Note that the skiver peak has been stiffened using hardboard, seen on its left edge, while the fully cloth covered peak is softer and is most probably stiffened by leather. *Private Collection.*

A mid-wartime Bates Hatter's cap from an Officer holding the rank of Group Captain. His rank is denoted by the patent leather peak and single row of gold-wire oak-leaf. This cap shows a pronounced saddle shape. *Private Collection.*

An early wartime Bates Hatter's Group Captain's cap. By comparing with the mid-war example we can observe how style and appearance can differ, even from the same Outfitters. *Courtesy of Tod Rathbone. Rathbone Museum of World War II Aviators.*

Close-up detail of a Group Captain's oak-leaf rank distinction and patent peak. *Private Collection.*

Group Captain and Senior Ranks

While their rank device differed, peak configuration for the ranks of Group Captain and higher was very similar, using a black patent leather peak and rim, with green skiver underside. The patent's varnished surface can get crazed or cracked over time, as does the rim to a small extent.

The addition of peak mounted oak-leaf served to denote rank, which in the case of Group Captains was a single row, while for Air ranks was a double row. An important point worth noting is that the oak-leaf of the RAF ranks has a sharper look to the more rounded "oak" leaf of the Royal Navy.

Rank Device

The rank device for Junior Officers consisted of a gilt metal eagle which surmounted an embroidered gold-wire wreath. The eagle, facing to the left when the cap was worn, was positioned below a dominant King's crown. The crown was also embroidered with gold-wire and used coloured thread with red velvet to show detail.

The entire device was mounted onto black or dark blue felt, which either had a black canvas/oilcloth, cotton or waxed paper covered backing. A comparison of these backings can be viewed in the Royal Navy chapter. The rank device was sewn directly onto a removable black woven band.

Dimensions of the badge varied slightly from maker, where the wreath was wider or the crown taller. However, the overall dimensions were not overly different.

Device dimensions (Jnr Officer example):
Length (exc. Backing) 6.4cm.
Width (exc. Backing) 6.2cm.

Device dimensions (Grp. Capt Officer example):
Length (exc. Backing) 6.4cm.
Width (exc. Backing) 6.5cm.

In 1944 an "economy" version of the cap badge was introduced as a temporary measure, resulting from a lack of precious wartime materials. The badge was of a similar style to that of the standard badge, albeit being comprised totally of gilt, with black cloth edging and similar backing.

Economy device dimensions (Jnr Officer example):
Length (exc. Backing) 6.2cm.
Width (exc. Backing) 6.cm.

The "economy" example shown has an orange hessian backing panel which displays the gilt split-pins of the metalwork. In most cases this would have been covered with an additional piece of black oilcloth.

A collector must take care not to confuse an "economy" cap badge with that of the beret. Although at first glance the beret badge appears identical, it is considerably smaller in size at 5cm x 5cm, while its metal components are more fused together and lack spacing between them.

A beautiful and rare example of a Senior RAF Officer's peak cap. The combination of the cap badge and peak detail denotes Air rank. This cap is also unusual as it features white stitching around the crown as opposed to piping, which is more common on such caps. *Courtesy of Tod Rathbone. Rathbone Museum of World War II Aviators.*

An early attributed example of a Senior RAF Officer's peak cap, as can be seen from the peak size and shape, as well as from the narrow chinstrap. *Private Collection.*

Air rank peak detail displaying a double row of gold-wire oak-leaf mounted to a black patent leather peak. *Courtesy of Tod Rathbone. Rathbone Museum of World War II Aviators.*

A typical Royal Navy Senior Officer's peak. Note the differences between that used on a Royal Air Force Officer's cap, and indeed also the pattern used on an Army Forage cap. *Private Collection.*

Two additional examples of the Officer's RAF device. Slight variations in style and components can be seen clearly. *Private Collection.*

A typical RAF Officer's cap badge. *Private Collection.*

An illustration of an RAF Chaplain's distinctive peak cap badge, used by Officer's including and below the rank of Group Captain. This style of badge remained in use, albeit with a Queen's Crown, for a significant period post-war.

The construction of the beret badge is as the "economy" cap badge. Note that the crown's ermine rim is a separate piece of white metal, while coloured enamel serves as jewel and ermine detailing. This example is quite an exquisite piece in its own right, and one can expect to pay upwards of £20 Sterling.

The Junior Officer cap badge was used by all RAF Officers, including the Volunteer Reserve, Medical Officers and Dental Officers. However, the cap badge used by Chaplains of the Royal Air Force differed somewhat.

Surmounted by an oversized embroidered crown, the black metal Maltese cross was superimposed onto gilt wings and displayed a centrally positioned gilt laurel wreath with the abbreviation, "RAF", which is similar to the cap badge of RAF Airman. The device was then mounted onto an extended oval shaped black felt backing, which served to include the crown.

The cap badge used by officers of Air Rank was similar in its overall appearance to that of Army General Officers. Surmounted by the Royal crest (lion & crown), the gilt eagle was centrally positioned over an embroidered laurel wreath, whilst the entire device was mounted onto a black felt ground. The badge backing was covered in light coloured paper or cloth and trimmed to be flush with the badge's outline. Dimensions can vary slightly.

The "economy" gilt RAF cap badge, introduced late war. The backing panels of these badges were as that used on the embroidered version. Be wary of the beret badge version that is notably smaller. *Private Collection.*

A close-up view of an Air rank Officer's cap badge. The overall dimensions and construction is similar to that of Army General Officers. *Courtesy of Tod Rathbone. Rathbone Museum of World War II Aviators.*

Device dimensions (Air rank example):

Length (exc. Backing)	6.5cm.
Width (exc. Backing)	5.5cm.

Band

A black mohair woven band, as used on Royal Navy peak caps, was passed around the body of the cap. The join was sewn together and positioned centrally so as to be covered by the rank device. Once fitted the band and rank device were not usually removed, and it was not uncommon for the band to be tacked to the cap in several places. However this seems to have been more for device alignment than securing the band to the cap permanently. Dimensions varied.

Dimensions:

Width 4.2cm /4.5cm/ 4.7cm.

Length 6 7/8	59cm.
Length 7 1/8	63cm.
Length 7 3/8	64cm.

Royal Air Force Officer cadets were designated by a white cloth band worn over the black mohair band.

Chinstrap

A black patent leather chinstrap was attached to the cap via side buttons, and could be length adjusted using the slides. The chinstrap was mostly worn over the peak, where it met the cap body allowing the rank device to be perfectly positioned above it. The width of mid-war chinstraps were wider at 1.3cm.

Chinstrap dimensions:

Length	33cm (approx.).
Width	0.9cm.
Side button slit	2.5cm.

The shape of the slide end can either be half crescent or diamond, and along with its dimensions, could depend on the outfitter or personal taste of the Officer.

A detailed view of the black mohair woven band. *Private Collection.*

A crescent slide adjuster from a typical RAF black patent leather chinstrap. Note the "orange peel" surface texture of the patent. *Private Collection.*

A diamond shaped chinstrap slide adjuster. *Private Collection.*

Flat black cloth covered RAF side button, similar to those used on R/N caps. *Private Collection.*

A close-up view of the rear backing, from a wartime flat black cotton covered side button. *Private Collection.*

Half crescent slide dimensions (mid-war caps):

Length	2.2cm.
Height	1.5cm.
(Chinstrap width	1.3cm).

Half diamond slide dimensions (pre/early war):

Length	2.2cm.
Height	1.2cm.
(Chinstrap width	0.9cm).

Some chinstrap examples have blackened (non-patented) rear sides, while others have simply been left the original leather finish. When catching the light the patent surface displays an "orange peel" texture, as opposed to modern leather chinstraps that have a plastic gloss look. Note the photograph showing the crescent slide.

Side Buttons

The side buttons were of a standard style, regardless of rank. They were flat in shape and covered in fine black cloth on their outer surface, whilst their underside was painted black metal. They were sewn directly onto the cap body using a hidden metal loop and do not appear maker marked.

Side button dimensions:

Diameter	1.3cm.
Width	0.4cm.

Lining

The lining set-up of all peak caps regardless of the branch was very similar, featuring a leather sweatband, often embossed with "Real Roan Leather." The sweatband measured 5cm in width. Apart from Service caps supplied by Bates Hatter, where the lining was green felt baize, the majority of caps used a blue satin lining that was mostly quilted and/or padded. Another marking used on sweatbands is "Real Calf Leather," although these are not as common as the Roan examples.

The lining's sweat protector was either made from oilskin that covered the entire top panel or merely a diamond area. A transparent sheet of celluloid was also used for the same purpose and covered the top panel. It was either sewn into the cap or removable. The maker's label was situated below the sweat protector or in some

Lining from a mid-wartime Group Captain's cap. While some Bates caps were fitted with a sweat protector, this example was not. An interesting detail shared with the Bates Fusiliers cap is the lack of metal eyelets on the air-vents. Note also the maker's imprint on the green baize. *Private Collection.*

The lining from an early wartime Group Captain's cap. Note the black air-vents and the difference in peak underside to that of the other Group Captain's cap featured. *Courtesy of Tod Rathbone. Rathbone Museum of World War II Aviators.*

Lining from an Air rank Officer's peak cap. The top features a padded lining with a full oilskin sweat protector. What is unusual is the lack of air-vents, which was not however a standard characteristic of the Outfitter. Made by Moss Brothers. *Courtesy of Tod Rathbone. Rathbone Museum of World War II Aviators.*

Lining from an early Air rank Officer's peak cap. Note the spiral padded lining, typical of many Senior RAF and R/N Officer's peak caps. Made by Hector Powe. *Private Collection.*

A padded cap lining without the addition of any sweat-protector. No maker's label. *Private Collection.*

A textured RAF sweatband displaying a blind embossed Real Roan Leather marking. *Private Collection.*

cases acted as the sweat protector in its own right, although some makers chose not to insert their label and/or a sweat protector. Bates Hatter cap examples exist with or without the addition of a sweat protector.

Warrant Officers

Peak caps used by Warrant Officer and below were constructed from visibly rougher wool and were not specified to be worn on active duty, which perhaps explains why there are so few KC W/O examples. Instead the *Cap, Field Service* was authorised.

The body and top of the peak cap was constructed from a lower grade barathea wool and can appear slightly darker in shade to the colour of that of the Officer Corps. Piping was situated around the crown, whilst the Sides were also made from four cloth pieces and left unpadded. Steel crown stiffeners were often used. A black woven mohair band ran around the cap body.

The peak consisted of patent leather with a black oilcloth rim, whilst the underside was a textured green material. Like on the Officer's cap it was to be fixed at a 45 degree angle and be no wider than 6.3cm. The chinstrap was in the R/N style, consisting

A padded cap lining fitted with a diamond oilskin sweat-protector. *Private Collection.*

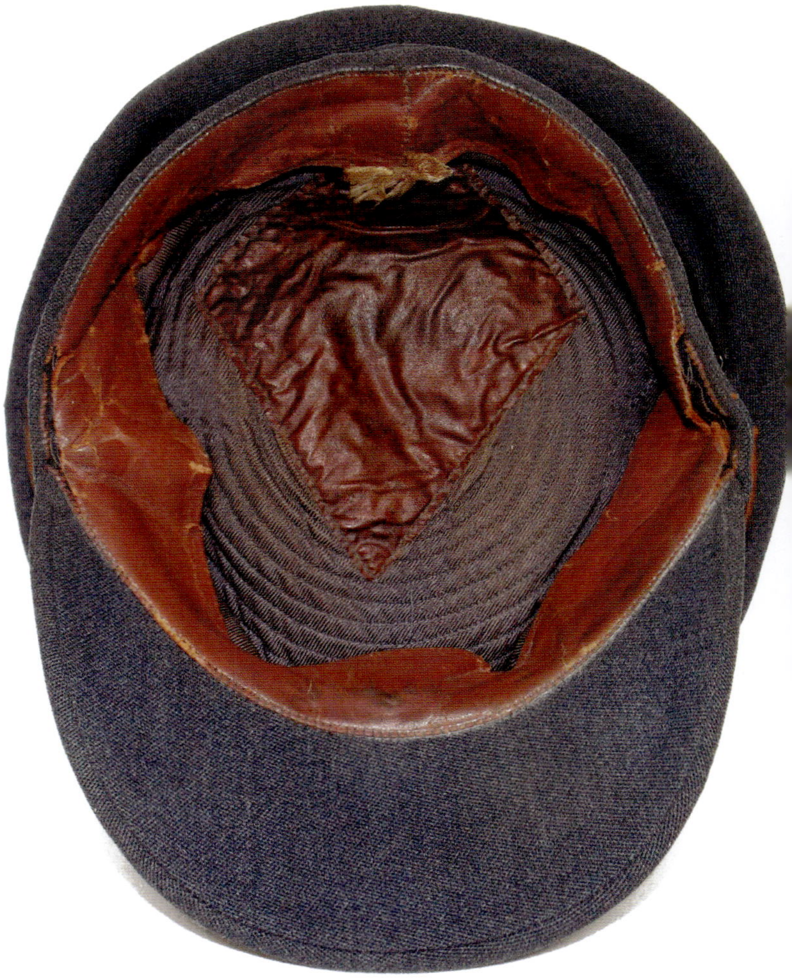

A cap lining fitted with a full top celluloid sweat-protector. The maker's label is for Austin Reed. Note the green skiver peak underside. *Private Collection.*

As with all NCO and enlisted men's peak caps, this Warrant Officer's cap was made from a lower grade material than that of the Officers, and were not usually private purchase. *Private Collection.*

of a black patent leather strap 0.9cm in width, and fitted with blackened metal rivets and adjusters. The chinstrap was fixed to the cap body using black cotton covered side buttons. The cap lining was standard plain cloth with a leather sweatband.

The W/O cap badge resembled that of a Junior Officer, however it was constructed from gilt and lacked the addition of a black cloth backing panel. Attached to the woven band using the pin and loop attachment, the tip of the wreath was meant to be positioned level where the cap band met the Sides. Some badge examples had a red cloth lining in the crown and areas painted black to define the device details.

Device dimensions:
Height 6.5cm.
Width 6.6cm.

RAF Ferry Command/RAF Transport Command

Set up in 1941, the Ferry Command branch of the Royal Air Force delivered factory new aircraft to the UK for immediate war service. In early-1943, it became part of the RAF Transport Command, which remained as such until 1967 when it was re-designated as the Air Support Command. Whilst the Ferry Command operated across the Atlantic with a limited role, the RAF Transport Command's responsibility included delivery of new aircraft and support operations, as well as transport missions.

Reflecting the exterior, NCO and Airman's cap lining was also of lesser quality material. *Private Collection.*

RAF W/O's cap badge, made of gilt. This particular example is unmarked and attaches to the cap by the pin & loop method. *Private Collection.*

The cap badge used by the Royal Air Force Transport Command. The RAF Ferry Command badge was near identical, albeit for the name difference on the scroll. *Courtesy of Tod Rathbone. Rathbone Museum of World War II Aviators.*

The cap badge consisted of a wreath surmounted by an Astral crown and superimposed by a flying eagle. Positioned centrally above the eagle was the RAF abbreviation, while below the eagle was positioned a scroll with the name of the specific organisation. Either *Ferry Command* or *Transport Command.* The entire badge was made of white metal and featured a blue enamel ground in the scroll and RAF abbreviation detailing.

The cap construction was similar to regular Royal Air Force or Royal Canadian Air Force caps, with the exception of being blue, as can be seen in this beautiful example of an RAF Transport Command peak cap. It is interesting, and perhaps not surprising, to note that the cap is from a Canadian Outfitter.

A beautiful and rare peak cap from the RAF Transport Command. *Courtesy of Tod Rathbone. Rathbone Museum of World War II Aviators.*

CHAPTER SIX

The Royal Navy

Royal Navy peak caps were used by all Officers and Non-commissioned Officers, for service and dress. While High ranking Officers used the same rank device as Junior Officers, it was the peak detail that served to highlight any distinction. It is interesting to observe that the vast majority of encountered Officers' peak caps were made by Gieves Ltd. The cap's overall appearance has remained largely unaltered since the Victorian age, apart from the most notable crown change, and minor changes to its style and dimensions.

A period photograph of a Royal Navy Lieutenant wearing the *Blue Cap* with a white cover. *Private Collection.*

Rank Structure of the Royal Navy

Admiral of the Fleet.
Admiral.
Vice-Admiral.
Rear-Admiral.
Commodore 1st class.

Commodore 2nd class.
Captain.
Commander.

Lieutenant Commander.
Lieutenant.
Sub-Lieutenant.
Skipper.
Midshipman.
Warrant Officer (commissioned).

Chief Petty Officer (Non-commissioned officer ranks).
Petty Officer.

Cap Body

Blue Cap

Officially designated the *Blue Cap*, the body and top were made from dark blue doeskin wool. Piping was situated around

Royal Navy ranks

1. **Flag Officers**
   Admiral of the Fleet.
   Vice-Admiral.
   Rear-Admiral.
   Commodore 1st class.

2. Commodore 2nd class.
   Captain.
   Commander.

3. Lieutenant-Commander.
   Lieutenant.
   Sub-Lieutenant.
   Skipper.
   Midshipman.
   Commissioned Warrant Officer.
   (With white cover fitted over cap top).

4. **Non-Commissioned Officers**
   Chief Petty Officer.

5. Petty Officer.

Royal Navy rank chart illustration.

A Royal Navy Flag Officer's *Blue Cap*. The double row of oak-leaf denotes the ranks of Admiral and that of Commodore 1st Class. *Private Collection.*

Plan view of a typical R/N cap showing the round shape of the top. *Private Collection.*

An example of a white canvas covered brass top stiffener, with a brass ferrule. *Private Collection.*

Close-up view of a brass stiffener showing the ferrule. *Private Collection.*

the top edging of the crown, between the band and Sides, and around the bottom edging of the body. From above the cap had a distinctively round look to its top section. *Blue Caps* tended not to have any air vents.

To maintain its shape, the Sides were sufficiently padded and a removable whalebone, brass or wooden (rattan or cane) stiffener was inserted into the top, closed by a brass ferrule. The fitting of a steel stiffener went strictly against Admiralty Regulations, due to its adverse effect on ship's compasses, and as such had not been used since 1916. The brass stiffener could either be raw metal or covered in white cloth and usually had a width of 0.5cm.

Some Officers, preferring the more stylish, and no doubt more practical, saddle shape look, tended to remove the crown stiffener and in some cases even the padding from the Sides. This made sense for certain postings where space was at a premium, such as in a submarine, but whatever the reason, these saddle caps did present a certain glamour or romance.

The body of the cap was stiffened using a double layered band of hessian, positioned between the sweatband and the cap body, and is usually covered by the cap lining, although it is sometimes

Close-up detail of the wooden stiffener. *Private Collection.*

A Lincoln Bennett made R/N Officer's cap displaying the saddle shape look. Note the slight variation to the chinstrap buckle style compared with the other examples featured. *Courtesy of Tod Rathbone. Rathbone Museum of World War II Aviators.*

An example of a wooden stiffener. The material is flexible, and is most likely rattan core or cane core. *Private Collection.*

A period photograph of Royal Navy Officers in summer dress. Mediterranean theatre. *Private Collection.*

A Royal Navy Flag Officer's *Blue Cap* fitted with the white cotton cover. *Private Collection.*

A Junior Officer's *Blue Cap* fitted with a white cotton cover, attributed to Lt. E.C. Titt, RNVR. *Private Collection.*

A R/N Captain's *Blue Cap* fitted with a white cotton cover. *Private Collection.*

A Junior Officer's *Blue Cap* without its device and mohair band. Note the width of the cover's band and the surface texture. *Private Collection.*

Overview of the white cotton pique top cover. *Private Collection.*

obvious if the lining is loose or was cut short. The hessian was to be 6cm in width and is an orange/yellow weave in appearance.

A white top cover, introduced in 1864, was to be worn in tropical climates and for summer season in home waters. The official summer season was from 1st May until the 30th September, inclusive. However from 1940 to 1946, the wearing of white covers (and the *White Cap*) in home waters was suspended. A khaki top cover was authorised to be worn with the Khaki uniform outside of home waters, at the instruction of a Senior Officer.

The cover was made from white pique cotton and sized 1.27cm bigger than the top. It consisted of a top panel, without piping, sewn to two Side pieces. A narrow band was sewn to the Sides, with a width of around 2cm. The cover was slipped over the top and the band inserted between the cap's woven band and body. The half seams were to then line up with the cap's front quarter seam and rear sweatband join.

A period photograph of a First World War Sub-lieutenant of the Royal Naval Division. *Private Collection.*

White Cap

The *White Cap* was introduced in 1922 and was to be worn in the same circumstances as that of the white cover on the *Blue Cap*. *White Caps* are rarely encountered or appear on the market, and so perhaps they were not popular with the Officers. The construction and style was identical to that of the *Blue Cap*, with the substitution of a white horsehair top without the addition of piping.

Khaki Cap

The *Khaki Cap* was similar in appearance to the cap and badge used by the Royal Naval Division in the First World War. The cap was authorised to be worn for shore operations, with the Khaki uniform, when an Officer was likely to be operating in front line areas. However this was replaced by the beret by 1944. There appears to be no specific details on the *Khaki Cap* but I assume this would have been similar to the army Service cap, used by the Royal Marines.

Peak Variations

Royal Navy Officer's peak caps of the Second World War are relatively easier to define, as all the wartime caps that I have encountered have "C" shaped peaks. Officially, peaks were specified to be at 45° in angle and 5.08cm wide at their maximum point.

For Junior Officers, the peak was patent leather with an underside of green skiver leather, and a patent leather rim. The underside was usually of a ribbed pattern or textured.

High ranking Officer's peaks had a patent leather rim and felt topside, matching the cap body, to which oak-leaf bullion was attached, denoting rank. The peak underside was also green skiver leather. Flag Officers wore two rows of gold oak-leaf.

Commodore 2nd class, Captain and Commander wore only one row. The oak-leaf was required to be 1.9cm in width.

Rank Device

Like the cap itself, the Officer's rank device had changed little since the Victorian age. The iconic Tudor GR crown, which we associate with the Second World War, was used from 1901 until it was replaced by the St Edward's Crown of Queen Elizabeth II, in 1953.

Royal Navy Officer's Khaki cap (Artist's impression).

An illustration suggesting how a Second World War *Khaki Cap* might have appeared.

Overview of a typical R/N black patent leather peak and rim. The underside was green skiver and could vary in textured appearance. *Private Collection.*

Admiral's peak cap fitted with white top cover.

Admiral's Blue Cap.

Peak comparison between two Gieves Ltd. Flag Officer caps. *Private Collection.*

A period photograph of a Royal Navy Captain. *Private Collection.*

R/N Cdr wartime peak detailing. Maker is Gieves Ltd.

Peak comparison between two Gieves Ltd. Commander caps. *Private Collection.*

Blue Cap attributed to Commander J.C.G. Martin, R/N, dating to 1944. *Private Collection.*

A First World War Royal Navy Officer's cap device. Note the differences to the wreath when compared against a World War II example. *Private Collection.*

A typical Royal Navy Officer's cap device. As with RAF badges, R/N badges could also vary slightly in style and proportion. *Private Collection.*

A quick identification chart showing the various backing materials used on World War II R/N and RAF embroidered cap badges. In most cases the hessian was covered by one of the other materials. *Private Collection.*

The device consisted of a gold-wire embroidered wreath which surrounded a white metal fouled anchor, surmounted by an embroidered crown. The lining of the crown was red velvet and varied in shade, from bright red to almost purple. Detail was added by coloured thread. Note the difference style from a World War I era R/N cap badge.

The badge was mounted onto black or dark blue backing felt, which either had a black canvas, waxed paper/cotton or cloth rear side.

Regardless of rank all commissioned Officers wore the standard cap badge, as well as non Executive Officers, of the Royal Navy Reserve, Royal Navy Volunteer Reserves, Fleet Air Arm, and Corps of Naval Constructors.

Actual device dimensions varied slightly from badge maker and even from cap to cap, compared to the official dimensions specified in the uniform regulations.

Device specified dimensions:
Length 6.3cm.
Width 8.5cm.

Device dimensions (Firmin & Sons example):
Length 7cm.
Width 7.9cm

Device dimensions (Geo. Kenning. & Son Ltd example):
Length 6.7cm.
Width 8cm.

The Royal Navy Chaplains' specific cap badge was of a similar pattern and configuration to that of the standard device, although the wreath was made from black velvet and trimmed in gold-wire.

Whilst at sea, a Royal Navy Chaplain would have served an entire squadron rather than being posted to an individual ship, which was the case with R/N Chaplain RJP Stewart MA, who was tragically lost on the Battlecruiser, HMS *Hood* in 1941.

The cap badge used by Officers of the Royal Fleet Auxiliary also varied slightly from the standard RN device, featuring a blue doughnut shaped ground with the abbreviation of R.F.A.

A period photograph of a Royal Navy Volunteer Reserve Officer, wearing his peak cap without a cover. *Private Collection.*

A *Blue Cap* attributed to Constr. Lt.Cmdr R.F. Lofft, Assistant Constructor, First Class, of the Corps of Naval Constructors. Notice that branch distinction is not displayed on the actual cap. The crazing on the peak has been caused by the sun and heat over time. Dated pre1944. *Private Collection.*

An extremely rare and unique example of a Junior Royal Navy Chaplain's peak cap. *Private Collection.*

Royal Navy cap badge distinction

(1) R/N, RNR, RNVR, Fleet-Air-Arm, Corps. of Naval Constructors.
(2) Chaplain.
(3) Royal Fleet Auxiliary.
(4) Royal Navy Transport.

Illustrations identifying various R/N cap badges. No.4 is World War I period.

The 1944 "economy" Officer's gilt cap badge. *Private Collection.*

The badge from a Royal Navy Chaplain's cap. The design and construction of the badge conforms to the standard R/N device, although features a black velvet wreath with gold-wire edging. *Private Collection.*

Detailing of the *Khaki Cap* cap badge. Usually found in bronze, it was later used on the beret. It is interesting also to note that the QC version remains in use. *Private Collection.*

superimposed in gold wire. The ground was edged in gold wire and surrounded a scaled down metal fouled anchor.

The RFA was set up in 1905 to act as a supply fleet to the Royal Navy, and during the Second World War its main role was to supply the essential materials and equipment needed to maintain a ship or a Fleet on station, such as food, ammunition and fuel.

In January of 1944 an "economy" version of the cap badge was approved, as a temporary substitute to meet the wartime shortage of gold wire used on embroidered cap badge. This construction style of badge was also used for various Petty Officer grades.

Economy device dimensions:
Length 7cm.
Width 8cm

Whilst the badge was mounted to a blue or black felt cloth backing, it was constructed from pressed gilt. The crown lining was filled with red velvet, with the ermine detail and anchor consisting of two separate pieces of white metal. Paint was used to provide further areas of small detail. The rear backing material was the same as that used on the embroidered device. Examples made by G.R. Gaunt & Son. Ltd. had the Royal Warrant and maker's details printed in white onto the backing panel, although most devices were not maker marked.

The *Khaki Cap* badge was similar to the "economy" version, being pressed metal, although it lacked a backing panel and was significantly smaller in size, measuring around 6cm long by 5cm high. The badge was specified to be made of bronze although the featured Firmin example is in white metal, with bronze attaching loops.

The Royal Naval Division cap badge of the First World War was fully bronze and attached to the cap using split pins or lug & pin, being roughly the same dimensions as the aforementioned badge. Later badges used a lug & pin attachment, and had a segment of red cloth to show the crown lining detail. The anchor

A First World War bronze cap badge for an Officer of the Royal Naval Division. The badge for Petty Officers was also bronze and reflected the embroidered version. *Courtesy of the Military Badge Collection.*

detail, crown ermine rim and backing plate were separate metal pieces. When the beret came into service the badge continued to be used, although was mostly made of gilt.

I have yet to see an actual example of a *Khaki Cap*, and as such it is unclear exactly what form the badge took compared to the First World War RND badge. However, the Second World War Royal Navy device style evidently has wider leaves at the base of the wreath while the RND wreath style is more oval. This would suggest that the later *Khaki Cap* badges took their style from the Second World War device.

Band

A black mohair woven band was fitted around the cap's body and was specified to be 4.4cm in width, however most wartime examples have a bandwidth of 3.7cm. The band's seam was positioned to be covered by the rank device, and its length was dependent to the cap's size. Once fitted the band and device would not have been removed.

Chinstrap

The Royal Navy also used a black patent leather chinstrap, attached to the cap side buttons. Again the chinstrap tended to be worn over the peak, positioned just below the rank device, as a buffer between peak and badge.

Chinstrap dimensions:

Length	33cm (approx.).
Short end length	7cm.
Width	0.9cm.
Side button slit	2.3cm.

The blackened brass hardware consisted of two flat buckles with rounded corners. A split-pin held the narrow buckle (1.3cm x 0.7cm) in position onto the short end of the chinstrap. Length adjustment was facilitated by the wide buckle (1.3cm x 1.3cm). The split pin was 0.4cm in diameter.

Some chinstrap examples had blackened (not patented) rear sides, while others had simply been left as the original leather. Similar to those of the RAF, R/N chinstraps also show an "orange peel" effect when light hits their patent leather surface.

Side Buttons

The side buttons were of a standard style regardless of rank. Constructed from metal, they were flat in shape and covered in black cloth on their outer visible side, whilst the rear surface was painted black metal. They are sewn directly onto the cap body using a hidden metal loop, and situated directly at the end of the peak. It appears these buttons were not marked. See the RAF example.

A R/N device with its black mohair woven band. Note the sewn seam hidden behind the badge. *Private Collection.*

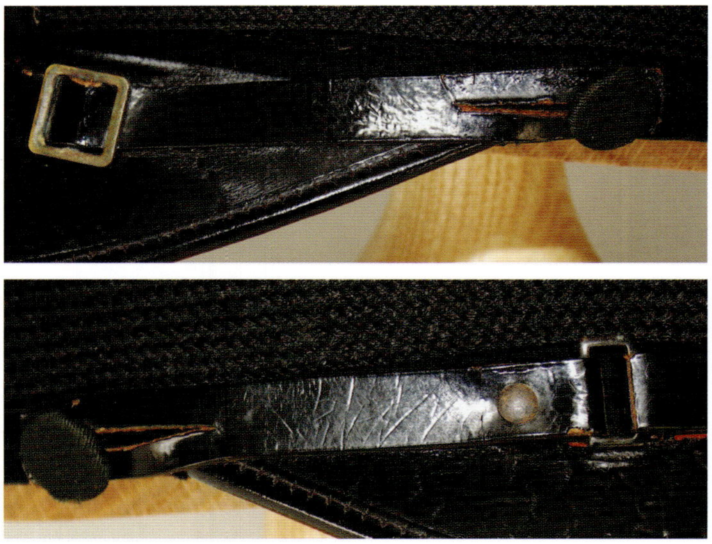

Detailing of a typical R/N patent leather chinstrap. The chinstrap itself consists of two pieces of leather and is adjusted by the black buckles. On this example the black paint has worn off to reveal areas of the brass metal. *Private Collection.*

Close-up of a typical R/N flat cotton covered side button, measuring 1.3cm in diameter. *Private Collection.*

Side buttons dimensions:

Diameter	1.3cm.
Width	0.4cm.

Lining

The lining in Royal Navy Officer's peak caps tended to mostly be plain blue satin, which in some cases was circular quilted, as is the case on most earlier Senior Officer examples, and examples made by Sanders & Brightman. Sweat protectors were rarely used but when encountered mostly consist of a diamond oilskin panel. The lining from the Royal Navy Chaplain's cap, whose Outfitter is unknown, dates from the inter-war/early war period.

Cap examples across all Branches could feature an additional velvet panel at the forehead area, where the peak joined the sweatband, acting as a slight comforter. A leather sweatband, measuring around 4.7cm in width, completed the lining configuration, which on certain caps was blind embossed with "Real Roan Leather." Some examples were made by Grayshott Stagers.

Outfitters' labels were either sewn onto the lining top section and/or printed directly onto the lining or sweat protector. Gieves Ltd. for example, featured a maker's label as well as an embossed Royal Warrant and logo in gold.

A typical lining style found on most R/N caps. This particular example is made by Gieves Ltd., identified by the gold embossed Royal Warrant, in addition to their maker's label. In some cases the embossed detail was worn away from wear or hair cream. *Private Collection.*

The spiral lining style, also from a Gieves Ltd. cap, used by many Outfitters. *Private Collection.*

An inter-war lining style. The maker is unknown. *Private Collection.*

Close-up details of the velvet softer positioned under the sweatband, at the peak edge. Note also the hessian body stiffener, half covered by the cap's lining. *Private Collection.*

A sweatband ink stamped with Grayshott Stagers, in this case from a R/N Commander's cap. *Private Collection.*

A detailed look at a wartime gold embossed Gieves Ltd. logo. Other Outfitters used a similar technique, such as Sanders & Brightman, which featured the KC centrally positioned over their name. *Private Collection.*

A rather nice group photograph of Petty Officers. If you look carefully at the front row, the Officer on the left appears to be wearing an "economy" badge. *Private Collection.*

A Chief Petty Officer's cap badge. The construction of P/O cap badges could either be that of the Officers, or of a lesser quality as highlighted. Quality can be most obviously noted in the red crown lining detail. *Private Collection.*

Similarly to the Officers, a gilt "economy" cap badge was used by Petty Officers. This particular badge denotes the rank of Chief Petty Officer. *Private Collection.*

Chief Petty Officer & Petty Officers

The badges used by Petty Officers was similar in construction to those of commissioned officers, however, the design consisted of a fouled anchor surrounded by a gold-wire ring or wreath, surmounted by an oversized crown. "Economy" badges were with either made from gilt, or inferior quality material, where the crown lining appeared as scarlet darned worsted wool.

The actual cap itself was of a similar construction and specification to that of the Officers, although material quality could vary considerably. Most P/O caps appear stubbier with a more upright looking peak.

Royal Marines

Although part of the Royal Navy, the Royal Marines adopted a similar rank system to that of the Army. Ranks of full Colonel and above used standard Army rank device on their caps, while Junior ranking Officers used the Royal Marine globe device. Officers serving with the Fleet Air Arm used their standard Service dress, as was the case with the highly decorated Major V.B.G. Cheesman RM.

Undress

The universal pattern Forage cap, which was occasionally worn at sea before the war, and worn as mess dress, consisted of a blue felt top with scarlet band and piping around the crown. The chinstrap was black patent leather and attached by gilt side buttons, while the peak was also patent leather. The badge was a two piece device consisting of the Royal crest positioned just above a globe, surrounded by a wreath and made of gilt, with an anodised silver or gilt globe, matching the tunic's collar badge. The side button displayed the Royal crest, as can be seen in the 1953 dated example.

This cap is typical of those worn by most P/Os. The "economy" badge would suggest the cap's date as being from 1944 with a rank of Petty Officer. Refer to the "economy" CPOs badge for comparison. *Courtesy of Tod Rathbone. Rathbone Museum of World War II Aviators.*

1938 lightweight pattern Royal Marine Officer's cap with fixed canvas top, dated 1953. Attributed to Lt. Colonel R. E. Burton RM. The original KC Royal Crest badge has been replaced with a QC stay-bright version, as the Officer served until the late 1960s. Note the army style peak detail. *Private Collection.*

Royal Marine Forage caps and ranks

(1) General Officers.
(2) Brigadier.
Substantive Colonel.
(3) Lieutenant Colonel.
Major.
(4) Captain.
Lieutenant.
2nd Lieutenant.
(Senior NCOs).
(5) **Caps fitted with white top covers.**
(Also giving impression of the 1938 lightweight cap).
(6) Gilt side button.

Royal Marine rank chart illustration.

A wartime example of a junior Royal Marine Officer's universal pattern Forage cap. The KC side buttons are gilt with a white metal Royal Crest. Leather has been used to stiffen the peak, with hessian for the body. The peak is patent leather with skiver underside. *Private Collection.*

Close-up view of the King's Crown side button, used by Royal Marine Officers until the mid-1950s. Full gilt was worn by other ranks. After that time a Stay-bright version was used. *Private Collection.*

As with the Royal Navy, in tropical and sub-tropical climates, as well as home summer season, a removable white cotton cover was worn over the top. In 1938 a lightweight peak cap was introduced, with a fixed white canvas top, although these caps were apparently not worn during the war.

Service Dress

Worn with the service dress uniform the Service peak cap was used until mid-war when the blue beret became more favoured. After the introduction of the beret, in 1943, the service cap was no longer used on parade. It should also be mentioned that General Service bronze side buttons were also used on Service cap.

The bronze Royal Marine globe device came in two parts. The globe and wreath was mounted to the band while the crown, surmounted by the lion, was attached to the bottom of the front quarter seam, of the cap's top. In the highlighted example the globe part has the lug & pin attachment, whilst the crown is fixed using split-pins.

Phased out in favour of the beret, the Royal Marine Service Cap was as that used by Officers of the army. This rare example possibly dates to the latter pre-war period, judging from the width of its chinstrap and its stiff shape. It is also worth noting that RM Officers of the Fleet Air Arm would have used a similar cap to this one. *Private Collection.*

The RM Service Cap device consisted of two pieces of browned bronze. In this particular case attachment to the cap is with split-pins as well as the pin & loop method. It is interesting to note also that the cap has been fitted with bronze General List side buttons. *Private Collection.*

The lining on this RM Service Cap is typical of any other army Service Cap. However, it features a large oilskin diamond sweat protector positioned over the maker's label. The cap has also been fitted with a non-removable metal top stiffener. *Private Collection.*

A Junior grade Merchant Marine Officer. Wartime. *Private Collection.*

A weathered Merchant Navy cap badge sewn to its original woven band, dating from the early-1950s. *Private Collection.*

The Merchant Navy

The Merchant Navy was and still remains the official designation for the British commercial registered shipping fleet. During the Second World War the main responsibility of the MN was on convoy duties during the infamous Battle of the Atlantic, and by the end of the war 30,000 men had been lost.

The uniform used by MN Officers was very similar to that of the Royal Navy, albeit with unique cap badge, rank insignia and buttons, which can be seen in this photograph dating from 1940. The cap construction and style was that of the universal *Blue Cap* pattern, which could be fitted with a removable white cotton top.

The cap badge consisted of a red felt oval edged with thick gold-wire, surrounded by a gold embroidered wreath, and surmounted by the MN crown. Superimposed onto the red felt was a metal anchor. The whole device was mounted onto black felt with the same backing as the regular R/N device. The badge was then sewn onto a black mohair woven band. The wreath shape of wartime badges and those of the 1950s were more oval in shape compared to most later examples, which resemble the wreath layout and shape of the Royal Navy.

Peak caps for Captains was identical to those worn by other officers, although the peak displayed a single row of gold embroidered oak-leaf. MN caps were supplied by various Outfitters, as well as those that supplied the Royal Navy, such as Gieves Ltd.

HM Customs & Excise, and the Waterguard

Part of HM Customs & Excise, the Waterguard, as their name suggests, implemented the duty of the HMCE at the sea entry points, which included checking for illegal imports and unpaid duties. The uniform and peak cap for all ranks of Preventive Officer was similar to that of the Royal Navy. The chinstrap was patent leather with blackened metal hardware and was attached using black side buttons displaying the crown. A white top cover was authorised for summer season, however when the Royal navy adopted the white vinyl top in 1956 the Waterguard followed suit.

The Waterguard cap badge, worn from 1912 until 1949, consisted of an embroidered crown surrounded by a gold-wire wreath, with a black felt backing. When it was replaced, the badge became more consistent to the Royal Navy Officer's device, and featured a metal portcullis surmounted by an embroidered crown positioned inside an embroidered wreath. In 1952 Chief Preventive Officers were distinguished by a single row of oak-leaf mounted to the peak, in the style worn by Merchant Navy Captains.

The cap badge used by HM Customs & Excise consisted of an embroidered crown surmounting a double bordered oval. In the centre of the inner oval was the Royal Cypher while below that read "CUSTOMS" in gold. The backing panel used black felt, while the device was made up of red felt, coloured thread and gold-wire.

Coast Guard

The cap badge style used by Officers of the Coast Guard was similar to that worn by Officers of the Royal Navy. For Junior

An illustration of the rare embroidered Waterguard cap badge. Pre-1949.

An illustration of a wartime HM Customs & Excise cap badge.

A typical example of a size label found on wartime era peak caps. The label was usually stuck near the sweatband's sewn seam. *Private Collection.*

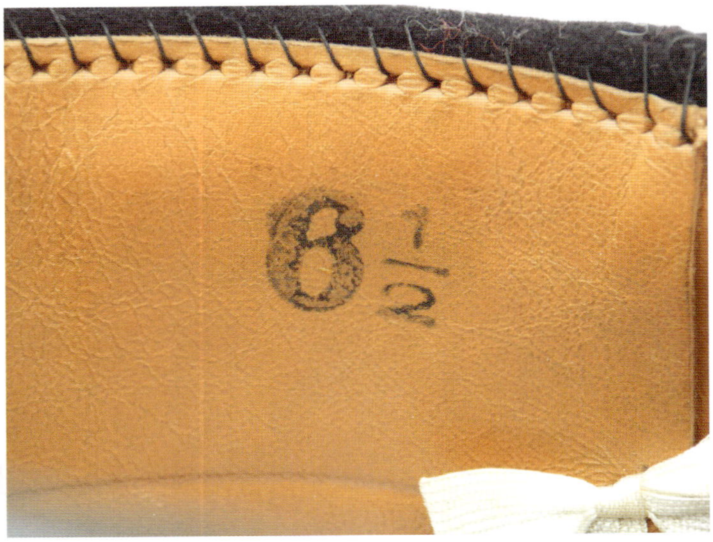

An example of the ink stamped size marking, usually positioned on the sweatband. *Private Collection.*

A gilt cap badge used by Junior Officers of the Coast Guard. *Private Collection.*

Officers the badge consisted of a rope textured oval frame surrounding a centrally positioned "CG" abbreviation. The device was surmounted by a crown. An example of which can be seen in the following image.

For Senior Officers the cap badge was identical to that of the Junior Officer, also being of gilt, albeit with the addition of an oak-leaf wreath. The wreath shape followed the oval, although was not as spread out as that used by the R/N. The appearance is more reminiscent of the Merchant Navy device featured earlier.

Sizes

As sizing is relevant to all branches, I have thought it wise to add this section to the end of this chapter, to avoid unnecessary repetition. Second World War peak caps came in a variety of sizes, however those most commonly encountered are of the size 55.

6 5/8:	53cm.
6 3/4:	54cm.
6 7/8:	55cm.
7:	56cm.
7 1/8:	57cm.
7 1/4:	58cm.
7 3/8:	59cm.
7 1/2:	60cm.

Whilst size markings were not always displayed, some Outfitters discretely wrote it in pencil onto the sweatband, used ink stamps or attached a small printed label.

CHAPTER SEVEN

Commonwealth Peak Caps

Upon the outbreak of war in 1939 volunteers from all corners of the British Empire and the Commonwealth answered the call to arms. Hundreds of thousands of Australians, Canadians and New Zealanders, to name but the most obvious, served in each theatre with their respective armies, navies and air forces, along side their British counterparts.

At first glance the uniforms and peak caps of the Commonwealth armed forces seem identical to those of the United Kingdom, however, on closer inspection many signs can help tell them apart. These details were due to national identity and local Outfitters, which gave these caps their own style and characteristics.

It should also be noted that as the materials, construction methods and certain standard components were as those used on British caps, you should refer to the relevant Branch chapter for a more detailed break down. As such this chapter is intended to be an introduction and overview, highlighting the main differences and features to look out for.

Australia

RAAF

Starting with the most obvious example first, the Royal Australian Air Force. Other than the distinctive dark blue coloured barathea used by the RAAF since the 1920s, the peak cap construction and style was almost identical to that of the Royal Air Force. Interestingly the RAAF still use the dark blue coloured uniform. The rank device was consistent to that used by the RAF.

The side buttons were blackened metal or black plastic, and displayed the RAAF motif, similar in style to those worn on the tunic. At some period after the Second World War the buttons were changed to gilt and Stay-bright.

RAN

Royal Australian Navy peak caps are almost identical to those used by the Royal Navy, and in fact in many instances were acquired from British Outfitters, or *Theatre made* to coin the U.S. term. Subtle differences do exist on local Australian made caps.

Army

The peak caps used by the Australian Military Forces was again similar to that used by the British Army, and while Senior Officer's cap rank insignia remain unchanged, standard cap badges were specific to a particular Australian regiment or corps.

The cap side buttons were either bronze, gilt or blackened metal, and depict the Australian land mass surmounted by the KC, surrounded by the text, "Australian Military Forces," as can be noted more clearly in the next chapter's side button material chart.

An example of such a cap is this Brigadier's Service cap. The cap features a fixed wire crown stiffener, as well as a removable clear transparent plastic sweat protector that covers the entire top section. The brass air-vents are painted brown on the face side, while the side buttons are black metal as mentioned above. The chinstrap slides are interesting as they have one thin discrete sewn seam, as opposed to most British caps that are thicker with two seams. The rank device is standard and is supported by a leather stiffener, as is the cap body.

The unique black side button worn by the RAAF. *Courtesy of Tod Rathbone. Rathbone Museum of World War II Aviators.*

This beautiful cap is typical of Royal Australian Air Force Officer's peak caps. In Britain especially, they are fairly uncommon and as such tend to command a higher price than their RAF counterparts. *Courtesy of Tod Rathbone. Rathbone Museum of World War II Aviators.*

A rather large sized Australian Military Forces Colonel/Brigadier's Service cap. Refer to the side button materials chart for a detailed view of the button. *Private Collection.*

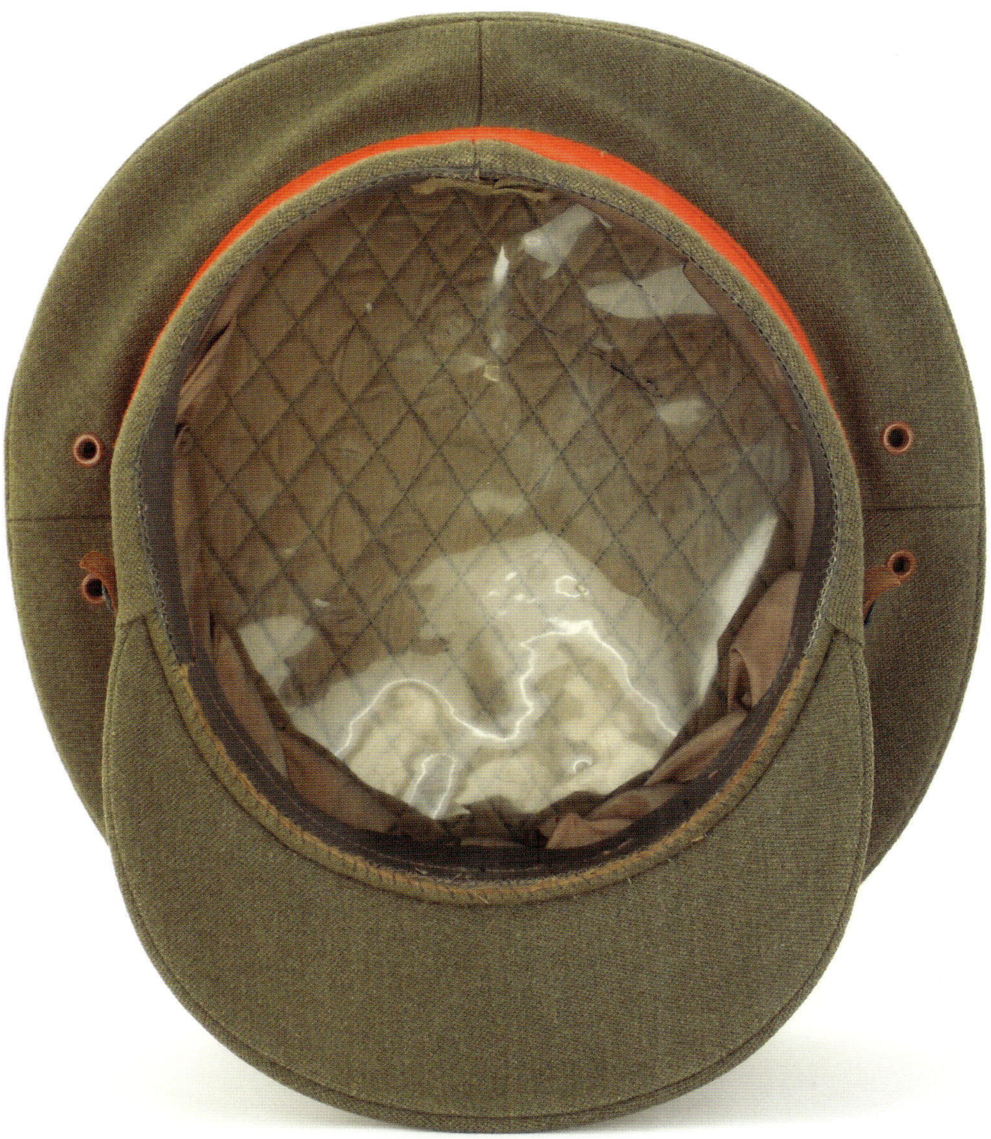

Quilted lining from a Australian Military Forces Senior Officer's Service cap, featuring a celluloid sweat protector. *Private Collection.*

Unusual and distinctive clay coloured air-vents from an Australian Military Forces peak cap. This is a prime example of an Outfitter incorporating their personal touch to what essentially is a standard cap pattern. *Private Collection.*

A slightly moth damaged RNZAF Officer's peak cap, missing its chinstrap. Attributed to Pilot Officer Rowan Jackson, who was sadly lost in 1943. The cap dates to October 1942 and is possibly British made. *Private Collection.*

A RNZAF Officer's side button, identical to those of the RAF. *Private Collection.*

Lining from the RNZAF Officer's peak cap. Note the skiver peak and quilted lining with oilskin protection. Unknown maker. *Private Collection.*

A canvas covered cap top stiffener with metal ferule, found in an RNZAF cap. *Private Collection.*

New Zealand

RNZAF

The Royal New Zealand Air Force Officer's peak caps are as those of the RAF. The highlighted example has a cloth covered leather peak with green skiver underside, while the body and badge area have hessian stiffening. The side buttons are the standard flat style and covered in black fine cloth, sadly the leather chinstrap is missing on this example.

The cap's Sides are padded at the frontal areas and the cap has a removable white canvas coated wire crown stiffener inserted. The top section of the cap lining is quilted and covered in an oilskin protector.

RNZN

As for the Royal Australian Navy.

Army

Whilst cap badges and side buttons displayed national identity the cap construction was of the universal British style, as can be seen in this example. Although locally produced caps can exhibit subtle variations.

A New Zealand Army Officer's Service Cap. Note the cloth texture on this particular example compared that of a British Service Cap. *Courtesy of Tod Rathbone. Rathbone Museum of World War II Aviators.*

Canada

RCAF

Peak caps used by the Royal Canadian Air Force were constructed using the same materials as regular Royal Air Force Officer's caps, and thus in most cases displayed an identical style. However, it must also be stated that RCAF examples exist that exhibit certain local characteristics. Note the highlighted peak material and wicker stiffener. An interesting side note: World War II era USN Officer's frame caps also used a similar wicker construction.

While the badge consisted of a gilt eagle (flying leftwards when the cap was worn), surrounded by a gold wire embroidered wreath and surmounted by the King's crown, the black felt border took a distinctly oval shape and/or was rounded off at the edges, compared to the appearance of a standard RAF device whose border was cut short and sharply to the device.

Furthermore we must also look at the side buttons. Whilst some caps used the standard flat black cloth covered style, examples also exist where the side buttons were slightly oversized at 1.6cm in diameter, dome faced and made from black Bakelite, which can be noted in this superb cap example.

It should also be mentioned that a third less common cap button was used, with a convex stud like appearance. The button was made of metal and covered in black cotton over a tan cloth lining, with a depth of 0.7cm and a diameter of 1.3cm. This button style can be seen in the well worn RCAF cap example, as well as on the RAF Transport Command peak cap, in the RAF chapter.

If we take this worn example, the cap features piping around the top edging instead of the white stitching. A non-removable crown stiffener serves to maintain that sharp disc appearance. The Sides are padded with blackened metal air-vents, 1cm in diameter, positioned either side of the rear seam. The black woven band is 4.3cm in width, while the body is stiffened using hessian. The lining features a diamond sweat-protector situated over the makers' label.

Concerning issues of lining, this really fell upon the individual Outfitters themselves. Usually, however, RCAF caps had an oilskin sweat protector covering the entire top section of the lining, or in lesser cases a diamond panel of the same material. Canadian maker's details or labels tended to be displayed quite predominantly.

Some caps also featured several sets of blackened metal air vents positioned on the sides and rear, as can be seen in the

A period photograph of a Royal Canadian Air Force Pilot Officer. *Private Collection.*

Wicker used as the cap body stiffener, opposed to hessian. *Private Collection.*

Cardboard or soft hardboard used to stiffen the peak. *Private Collection.*

The two styles of cap badge felt borders used on RCAF Officer's caps. These examples, together with the RAF devices featured earlier, also serve to show various stages of condition, resulting from age and quality of storage. *Private Collection.*

This saddle shaped Officer's cap has seen better days, but regardless to its condition, it displays the key characteristics of RCAF caps. Note the ribbed style to the woven band and the plain black somewhat oversized plastic side button. Due to bad storage the cap has darkened from mould and the gold-wire shows greening. It is also missing the left section of its chinstrap, as well as the left side button. *Private Collection.*

A close-up view of the black Bakelite RCAF side button. *Private Collection.*

This beautiful RCAF cap displays the same features as the saddle example, although the quality of the badge and condition are outstanding. It is also interesting to observe that the device is cut as those of the RAF. *Courtesy of Tod Rathbone. Rathbone Museum of World War II Aviators.*

A profile view of the previous RCAF cap. Note that the side buttons on this cap are of a similar size to the cloth covered versions. In contrast, the plastic button used on the saddle cap is larger. *Courtesy of Tod Rathbone. Rathbone Museum of World War II Aviators.*

This particular well worn RCAF cap exhibits piping around the crown and stud side buttons. The chinstrap is also interesting as it features metal buckles instead of the leather slides. Although an original feature to this specific cap, this chinstrap characteristic tends to be associated with RAF NCO's peak caps. *Private Collection.*

The less common RCAF black cloth covered stud side button, measuring 0.7cm in depth. *Private Collection.*

Thick textured oilskin lining. This cap also features a dual set of air-vents, positioned on the sides and at the rear. *Private Collection.*

A non-padded lining featuring a diamond shaped oilskin sweat protector, with the maker's label situated underneath. The sweatband features a leather reinforced strip at the forehead area, and together with the lining shows evidence of dampness. *Private Collection.*

saddled shaped example, and in some cases their bodies were stiffened using wicker. A stiffener was also positioned behind the cap badge area.

RCN

The uniform of the Royal Canadian Navy was identical to that worn by their Royal Navy counterparts, although lining characteristics and overall styling flair depended on the local Outfitter. RCN buttons, for the most part were flat and covered in black cloth, but in some instances textured half dome black Bakelite buttons were used, although these seems to be more the case during the 1950s. As with the RCAF, convex side buttons were also used.

On the highlighted example the peak is patent leather with an oilcloth rim and green skiver underside. The chinstrap is the standard pattern while the side buttons are Bakelite as stated above. The cap lining features a diamond shape sweat-protector over the maker's label, and situated over a blue lining in the spiral pattern.

Canadian Army

Peak caps used by Officers of the Canadian army differed little from those of the British, and as with Australian caps the difference was most obviously seen through the cap badge and side buttons, which for the most part were either specific to a Canadian unit or were "Canadianised" with the maple leaf and such symbols of national identity.

A detail which can be seen is this quite unique and intriguing U.S. Medical Officer's peak cap. The Officer joined the Royal Canadian Army Medical Corps, no doubt at the start of the hostilities, ordering his peak cap from Scully. When the United States entered the war he then transferred over. What is most interesting is the fact that he kept this cap and only replaced the cap badge.

An example of a Royal Canadian Navy Officer's cap made by Hamilton Uniform & Cap company. Although missing its rank device, it shows how the join of the woven band would have been hidden. *Private Collection.*

A close-up view of the oilcloth rim texture from the featured RCN cap. *Private Collection.*

It is interesting to note that this particular RCN cap exhibits air-vents, unlike those of the British R/N. The side buttons are also dome shaped textured Bakelite, a feature unique to Canadian caps. *Private Collection.*

Spiral padded lining from a RCN cap. Note the diamond shaped oilskin sweat protector.
Private Collection.

A unique and rare U.S. Medical Officer's Service cap. The Officer volunteered for the RCAMC, before transferring to the U.S. Army, interestingly keeping his original cap with side buttons. This cap can be confidently dated to within the period of 1939-1941, and thus it's genetic make-up can be used as a means for comparison. *Courtesy of James Katzenstein.*

An example of a "Canadianised" Army Service Cap side button. In this case from the Royal Canadian Army Medical Corps (RCAMC). *Courtesy of James Katzenstein.*

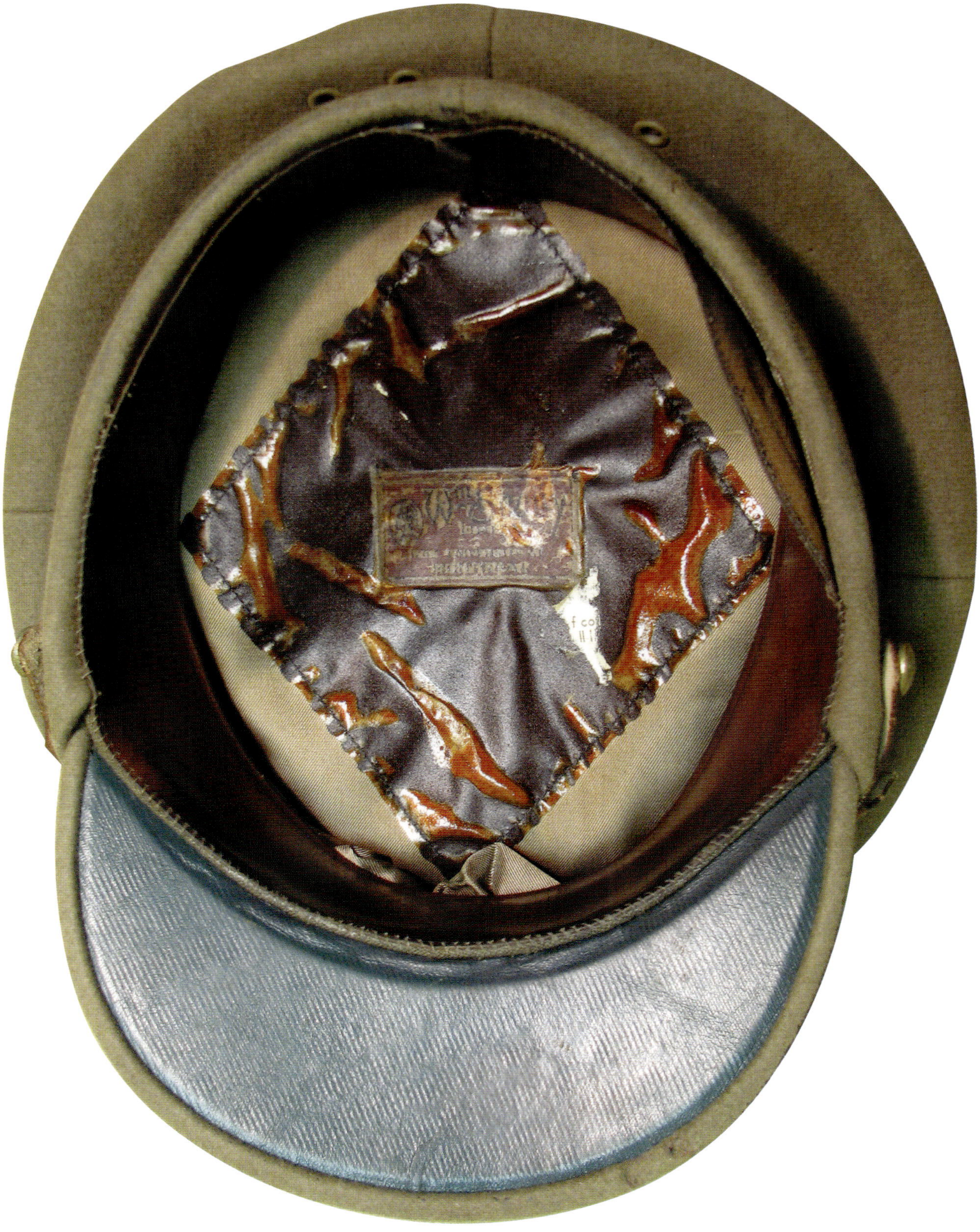

The lining from the RCAMC cap, showing a green skiver peak and oilskin diamond sweat-protector. Note also the fine felt appearance of the cloth which, in conjunction to the wide chinstrap, is consistent to the 1939 RAPC Gieves Ltd. cap featured in Chapter 4. *Courtesy of James Katzenstein.*

A typical example of the cap used by the South African Air Force. Style and construction is of the universal pattern. *Courtesy of Tod Rathbone. Rathbone Museum of World War II Aviators.*

A close-up look at the gilt cap badge used by Officers of the SAAF, attached usually with the pin & loop method. *Courtesy of Tod Rathbone. Rathbone Museum of World War II Aviators.*

South Africa

SAAF

The peak cap used by Officers of the South African Air Force was that used by the army, being the universal Service cap, matching the Officer's Service dress uniform. Caps were either locally made or from a British Outfitters. The cap buttons were bronze while the cap badge was gilt and consisted of a flying eagle looking towards its left, surrounded by a wreath and surmounted by a crown. Below the wreath is a scroll with the abbreviations, S.A.A.F. and S.A.L.M. written.

South African Army

Peak caps used by the South African Army were similar to the standard British Service caps. Side buttons and cap badges were specific to a particular regiment, while slight variations of style and materials depended on the Outfitter.

A British made peak cap from the Palestine Police Force, featuring a white metal cap badge and side buttons, conveniently dated to 1941. Although not strictly military this cap serves to document that military and civil authorities in other areas of the British Empire and Commonwealth used such caps, albeit with specific badges and buttons. *Courtesy of James Katzenstein.*

Miscellaneous

Other parts of the Commonwealth who volunteered to fight for the Allies included Ceylon, India, Jamaica and Rhodesia. The majority of Commonwealth countries used the standard service uniform of the British, with shoulder titles for the RAF and Royal Navy.

Army units also used the standard Service dress and cap albeit with specialised badges and buttons, for their respective regiments and countries. These marks of identity were either locally made or sourced from British Outfitters and suppliers, which can be noted on this fine example of a wartime Palestine Police Officer's cap, made by G.A. Dunn of London.

CHAPTER EIGHT

Post-war Peak Caps & Dating a Peak Cap

Post-war Peak Caps

To the untrained eye, the overall appearance of wartime and post-war peak caps seem nearly identical, especially in the case of those caps produced in the decade or so following the end of the Second World War.

In basic terms however, post-war caps can fall into two easy to identify categories, pre-1960/1970s and post-1960/1970s. In the case of the former, specifying a cap to a particular date within that period can be somewhat easier than the latter, due to the material of the cap's components, careful study of the cap badge and observing the shape of the crown.

Before you read any further, I would like to clarify that this chapter is by no means comprehensive, but instead serves as an overview supporting the main theme of this book. I would also like to add that I have grouped the post-war and dating sections together, as the two are somewhat interlinked.

Army: Dress

Cap Body

1946-1960s
Forage caps, or Dress caps as they became more commonly known, of the immediate post-war years were of a similar style and construction to those used just prior to and during the Second World War.

1960s - Present
The majority of all caps from this period display the saddle shape, with the main exceptions coming from the Guard Regiments. From the 1960s plastic was used to stiffen the band and badge area. Note the absence of any air vents. You should also take into account that the colour of Dress caps used by Line Infantry was of a very dark blue, almost black, however, in the 2000s some caps exhibit more of an obvious blue, which can be noted in this Junior Officer's Dress cap example from pre-2007.

Peak

1946-1970s
As wartime. Caps were fitted with a peak consisting of a black patent leather topside and rim with green skiver underside.

1970s - Present
During the 1970s black glossy vinyl was used for both the peak topside and rim, while green textured vinyl was featured on the underside. Whilst the peak shape and style of all post-war Dress caps remained consistent to that used during the war, being a distinctly round "C" shape, most recent Junior Officer's caps tend to have a shorter stubbier peak, reflecting that of the Service cap. Regiment and rank distinction displayed on the peak also remains true to what was used during the Second World War.

Cap badge:

1946-1953
The cap badge used by all Officers was consistent to that worn during the war, which is covered in a previous relevant chapter. The exception to this were those regiments whose badges saw slight redesigns, a subject touched on later in this chapter.

1953 - Present
The change in crown design was no doubt the major difference with those cap badges worn pre-1953. Gilded metal, bi-metal or sterling silver tends to be most common on these caps.

The embroidered cap badges used by the ranks of substantive Colonel and above, have also changed little in style and overall construction, with the main difference being the use of the QC as opposed to the KC. The subtle varied styles of the QC together with a machine made feel can sometimes hint towards which era the cap is from.

A mid-1960s Field Officer's Dress cap from the Worcestershire Regiment, displaying Stay-bright side buttons and a patent leather chinstrap. During that period however the badge would have been that of the Mercian Brigade. *Private Collection.*

A post-1970 Field Officer's Dress cap from the newly amalgamated Worcestershire & Sherwood Foresters Regiment, also displaying Stay-bright side buttons and a patent leather chinstrap. The cap badge would have been that of the new WFR. *Private Collection.*

A 1971 dated officer's Dress cap attributed to Colonel A.R.G. Harrington, Commander of the RAOC, 1973. The cap features gilt side buttons befitting its rank. The chinstrap is patent leather. *Private Collection.*

Frontal view of the Colonel's RAOC cap showing the saddle shape look, typical of most post-war caps. *Private Collection.*

A Junior Officer's Dress cap to the Worcestershire & Sherwood Foresters Regiment. Note that the chinstrap is plasticised leather, while the side buttons are Stay-bright. This cap dates to the 2000s and is typical of current issue peak caps. *Private Collection.*

Note the difference in cloth colour between a 2000s Dress cap and that of the 1970s. *Private Collection.*

1971 dated Colonel's peak detail: Herbert Johnson.

Post 1970 Field Officer's peak detail: Herbert Johnson.

2000s Junior Officer's peak detail: Herbert Johnson.

Post-war Dress cap peak detail. The Junior Officer's example displays a vinyl peak and rim, while the other examples are patent leather. Vinyl was used in caps from the 1970s, although for Army Dress caps this choice of material is most noted on late 20th Century and early 21st Century examples. *Private Collection.*

An embroidered cap badge worn by Substantive Colonel and Brigadier, of a similar pattern and construction to that of wartime. This badge would also have used on the Service cap. *Private Collection.*

An embroidered Colonel's cap badge, with typical QC, dating to 1971. *Private Collection.*

Close-up detail of half crescent slides from two post-war Dress cap examples. The chinstrap in the left image is patent leather and shows "orange peel," while the one of the right is plasticised leather. *Private Collection.*

Stay-bright buttons were used on most peak caps from the 1950s, including Service caps. *Private Collection.*

Gilt was still used on all Senior Officer's Dress caps post-war, as can be seen from this Substantive Colonel's side button. *Private Collection.*

Chinstrap

1946-1970s

The appearance and construction of Dress cap chinstraps from this period are as mid-wartime.

1970s - Present

Black vinyl or plasticised leather has replaced the traditional black patent leather used on earlier caps. The dimensions and style of the slides also varies, although the vast majority display the half crescent shape.

Side Buttons

1946-1950s

Dress cap side buttons reflect those used during the war, being either gilt, white metal or blackhorn.

1950s - Present

Stay-bright was introduced during the 1950s which replaced the use of gilt for side buttons. However, Gilt was still used by Senior Officers. Furthermore specific regiments continued to use their white metal and blackhorn versions as they had done previously.

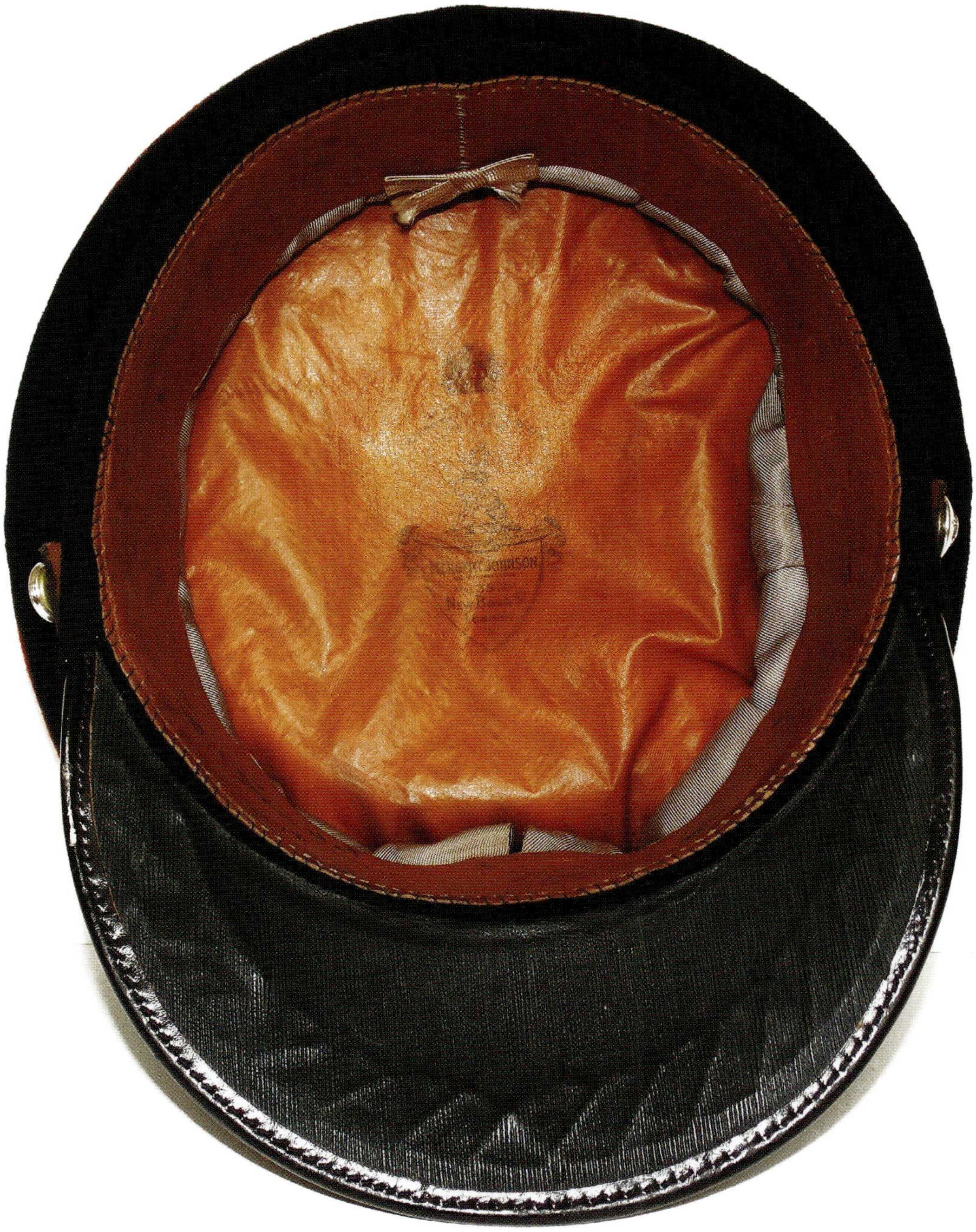

Lining from a 1960s Dress cap. Note its style and construction is very similar to wartime Dress caps. The oilskin sweat protector is in a good condition and has not become sticky and brittle as can be seen in the 1970s example. *Private Collection.*

The Real Roan Leather marking found on 1960s and 1970s peak caps, highlighting the fact that such markings were not restricted to wartime examples, or even Herbert Johnson made caps. *Private Collection.*

Lining

1946-1960s
As wartime.

1970s - Present
In general terms the lining of Dress caps has changed little over time, although during the latter post-war period light or dark coloured nylon was also used for the main lining material. Sweatbands can either be leather or imitation leather vinyl, which is most usual on modern caps. Blind embossed Real Roan Leather sweatbands are also common.

Lining from a 1970s Dress cap. The oilskin sweat protector has become stuck to the top's lining, and as was most usual, covered the whole top section but not the lining's Sides. *Private Collection.*

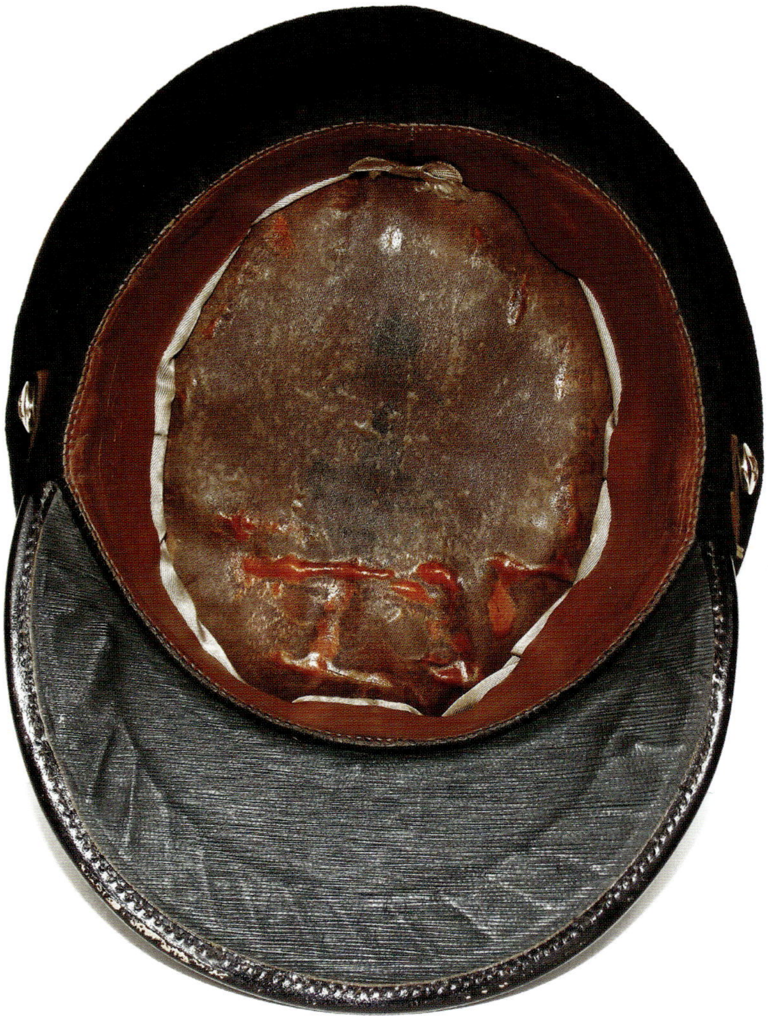

Lining from an early-1970s Colonel's Dress cap, fitted with the celluloid sweat protector as opposed to oilskin. The celluloid would have covered the top section only, and was either removable or sewn into place. As with the previous lining examples, the peak underside is green skiver. *Private Collection.*

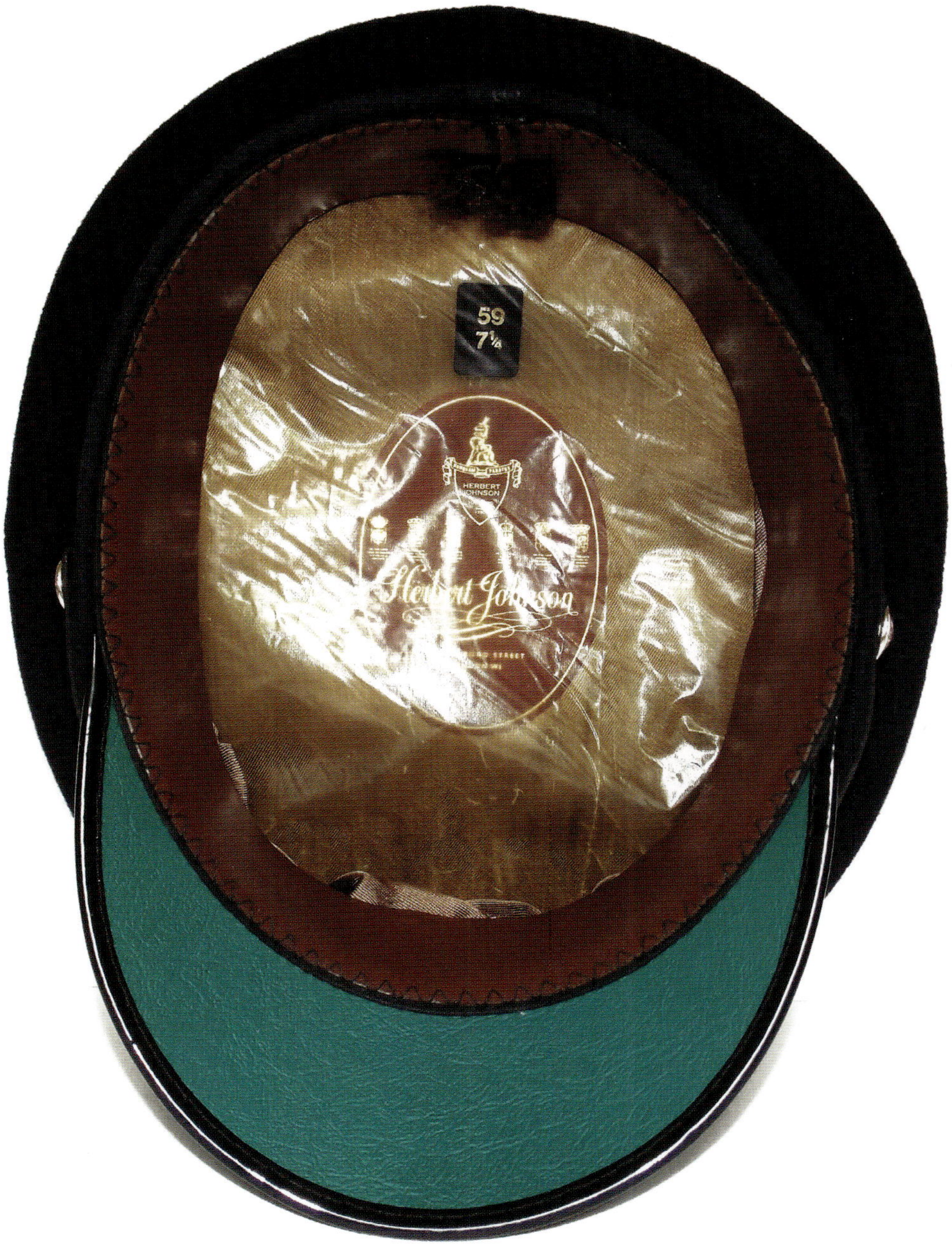

Lining from a 2000s Dress cap. The sweat protector is a type of transparent polythene, thinner to the somewhat rigid celluloid used previously. The sweatband is leather but appears more plasticised than those used in the 1970s. This lining is typical of the vast majority of current issue Army caps. *Private Collection.*

In the majority of cases the lining material is covered by a full top sweat protector. On older caps, from the 1960s and 1970s in particular, this was made of thin orange/red oilskin or celluloid. However celluloid and transparent polythene seem to be the material of choice for current issue Dress caps.

Army: Service

Cap Body

1946-1960s
The construction of post-war cap bodies was similar to that of wartime. Hessian was used to stiffen the band, and in some cases to stiffen the badge backing area.

1960s - Present
Caps dating from the 1960s tended to take a floppy or saddle shape appearance, as well as a shorter top overhang/bevel at the front, above the badge position. Whilst all post-war caps from this period lacked the piping between the band and the Sides, caps made by Herbert Johnson also tend to lack the crown piping detail.

Peak:

1946-1960s
Up until the 1960s, the peak size and shape conformed to those worn during the war.

1960s - Present
During the 1960s however, the peak shape became shorter and

Front view of the featured cap showing the badge positioning and shorter side bevels. Upon the Officer's promotion to Substantive Colonel, the WFR badge would have been removed and a red felt band added, together with an embroidered QC embroidered Royal crest badge. *Private Collection.*

distinctly rounded, when seen in plan view, a noted "C" shape. Regardless of this change the peak construction and full cloth covering remained unaltered.

Cap Badge

1946-1953
As for Dress caps.

1953 - Present
Post-war badges have changed little in overall construction and style, other than the main difference being the crown shape. The material and finish depended on the regiment but the badges tended to be bi-metal or Stay-bright. Subdued cap badges were made from dulled bronze and mostly appear black or dark brown. Attachment was either by slide or the lug & pin configuration, which was used on both Service and Dress caps. Embroidered cap badges are as for Dress caps.

Chinstrap

1946 - Present
The chinstraps used on post-war Service caps were as that of mid-wartime, consisting of brown leather with slide adjusters. The width was around 1.5cm.

An early-1960s saddled shaped Service cap, attributed to Brigadier R.G. Silk, who joined the Worcestershire Regiment in 1962 and later became Colonel of the amalgamated WFR regiment. Note the lack of crown piping and the side buttons befitting the Officer's rank. *Private Collection.*

Side profile view of the featured 1960s Service cap, showing the short style of the peak, rear bevel overhang, wide chinstrap, and distinctive saddle shape, typical of all post-war Service caps. The cap features Stay-bright Colonel's buttons, worn by all grades of Colonel, as well as Brigadier. *Private Collection.*

A typical post-war lining used from the 1960s. The shorter "C" shaped peak can be clearly noted. The sweatband is blind embossed, Real Roan Leather, while the lining is covered in orange oilskin. Note the position of the air vents. *Private Collection.*

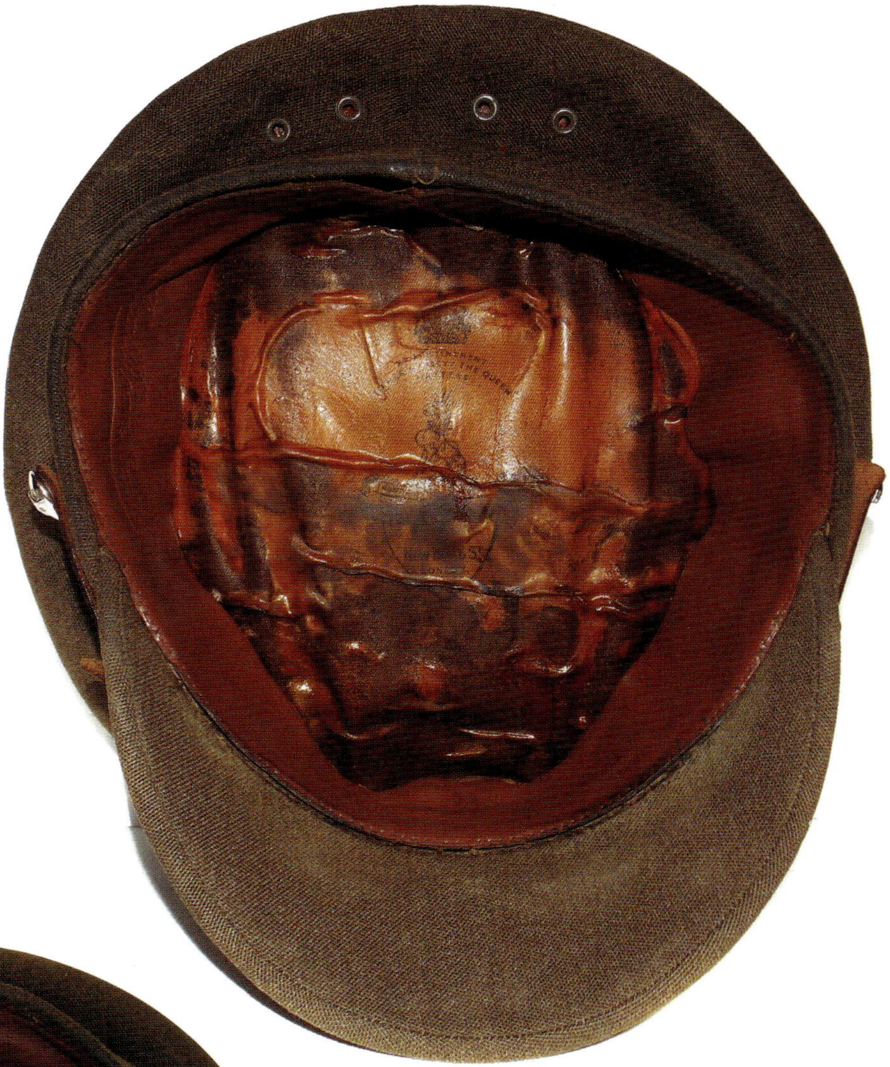

Another example of a post-war Service cap, dating to pre-1970. The oilskin sweat protector has split and become stuck together, revealing the pale cloth cap lining. A common occurrence with oilskin protectors. *Private Collection.*

A rear view of a post-war Service cap, highlighting the air vent position and detailing. *Private Collection.*

Side Buttons

1946-1950s
The side buttons were either bronze, white metal or blackhorn, as used worn during the war.

1950s - Present
From the 1950s Stay-bright was used instead of bronze, although as with the Dress caps, this did not affect specific regiments that used other button materials, such as The Rifles or Army Chaplains.

Lining

1946-1960s
As wartime.

1970s - Present
On most post-war Service caps, from the early part of this period, the lining tended to be made of a light coloured cloth. In the 1960s and 1970s, in most cases, this was covered in a thin dark orange oilskin sweat-protector, which covered the complete top section. It is interesting to note that this can become sticky over time and thus easily tears.

Later more modern Service caps prefer to use celluloid sweat-protector, while imitation leather can also be found for the sweatband, depending on the maker. Air vents should measure around 0.7cm in diameter and in most cases are positioned either side of the rear seam, on the Sides.

RAF

Cap Body

1946-1960s
The style and construction of RAF Officer's peak caps has changed little since the Second World War, but it was during the immediate post-war years that the piping detail around the top and the saddle shape became the predominant features.

1960s - Present
By the 1960s most caps had adopted the saddle shape, that is to say the cap top lacked the addition of a wire stiffener. The Sides also displayed a shorter overhang or bevel, while the top was not padded.

During the latter decades of the 20th Century plastic was used as well as hessian to stiffen the badge position, while cardboard,

Notice also the 1970s RAF cap's short styled bevel overhang, seen most clearly from the front. *Private Collection.*

hessian or plastic was used to stiffen the cap's body shape. However, although still encountered the current trend seems to lean away from the saddle shape, with wire stiffeners being re-used to maintain a smarter appearance.

Peak

Peak style remains consistent to those of wartime, but during the post-war period all caps favoured the "C" shape, while peaks used by Junior Officers from the 1960s to the present have a shorter more stubbed appearance. On an E.C. Snaith example, dating from the 1990s, the widest point of the peak measures 5.3cm.

Plasticised black leather or vinyl is used on later "issue" Senior Officer's peak caps for both the topside and underside of the peak. The difference depends on the Outfitter and the cap's intended use.

Cap Badge

1946-1953

During the years immediately preceding the war King George the VI was the reigning Monarch, and so the cap badge was that used shortly before and during the war.

1953 - Current

When Queen Elizabeth II became Sovereign the crown detail of the badge was changed to that of St. Edward's. The earliest examples of this crown resembled a swollen World War II crown, while from the 1960s to the 1990s the crown appears to have a fuller velvet cap, compared to current examples where the arches are more dominant and the velvet cap less bulbous.

The general style and construction of the badge remained nevertheless unchanged. A characteristic of all eras is the fact that the dimensions of the overall badge and fittings vary slightly, while the badge backing can be paper or cloth. A QC badge from a 1990s E.C. Snaith cap measures 6.8cm wide by 6.6cm tall, excluding the black felt.

Chinstrap

Pre-1970s

The general pattern of the RAF chinstrap has remained consistent throughout, and up until the 1970s the chinstrap was black patent leather with slide adjusters for sizing. During the war the chinstrap width widened and remained as such post-war.

A 1970s Hong Kong made Royal Air Force Officer's cap. As a typical post-war cap, it displays piping around the crown and is most obviously saddled shaped. *Private Collection.*

As with Army Service caps, the cap appears quite compact compared to wartime examples, evident from the shorter overhangs and peak shape. Features observed from the 1960s. *Private Collection.*

A mid-1990s British made E.C. Snaith Royal Air Force Officer's cap. Whilst also saddled shaped, the cloth material is slightly lighter weighted and the top lacks padding. The peak is also the shorter type. *Private Collection.*

Peak shape and style comparisons from two Junior RAF Officer's caps. The example on the left is larger and "D" shaped, dating to 1945, while the example on the right is shorter and "C" shaped, dating to 1992. *Private Collection.*

A 1970s Junior Officer's cap badge. Despite the obvious crown difference this cap badge design and layout has remained unchanged since before the Second World War. *Private Collection.*

A 1990s Junior Officer's cap badge. Note the subtle differences to the 1970s example as well as the fact that this badge appears "machine" made. *Private Collection.*

Post-1970s
As opposed to the "orange peel" look of earlier patent leather chinstraps, later leather chinstraps appear plasticised, or alternatively were made completely from black vinyl. The vinyl example featured comes from a 1990s era cap and is 1.6cm wide.

A crescent slide from a 1970s peak cap. The chinstrap is black plasticised leather and not patented. It is also interesting to observe that the vast majority of post-war RAF caps use crescent slides. *Private Collection.*

Side Buttons

1946-1960s
Post-war RAF side buttons tend to be flat and covered in cloth, identical to those used during the conflict, measuring 1.3cm diameter.

1970s - Present
During the latter part of the 20th Century, and into the 21st Century, cloth covered side buttons continue to be used, favoured by the more exclusive Outfitters. However, a cheaper alternative were the black textured plastic side buttons, designed to a similar specification and to emulate the cloth version. Refer to the R/N section that follows.

Lining

Pre-1970s
Up until the 1970s the cap lining was largely similar to that used during the war. Sweatbands were leather while sweat protectors were rarely featured.

1970s - Present
Man-made materials have become more commonplace on later caps, and so depending on the Outfitter and dress, the cap's sweatband could either be made of leather, or vinyl/leather effect. A leather sweatband from a 1990s Officer's service cap example measures 4.6cm in width.

The vinyl chinstrap from a 1990s peak cap. Despite the material the basic construction and style was as that of leather chinstrap examples. Current issue caps can either have a plasticised leather or vinyl chinstrap, depending. *Private Collection.*

A 1990s flat cloth covered side button. Whilst the style and dimension is consistent to previous era buttons, the material texture is finer and appears to be synthetic rather than cloth. *Private Collection.*

A 1970s flat cloth covered side button, displaying little difference in style and dimension to those of wartime. *Private Collection.*

Lining from a 1970s Junior Officer's cap. This cap was originally fitted with a rigid transparent polythene-like sweat protector, which is now only evident under the cap's Sides. The sweatband is actually imitation leather. *Private Collection.*

Close-up detail of the 1970s cap's sweatband and lining material. *Private Collection.*

Lining materials were again mixed, although more man-made fibres were used, such as Nylon, while nearly all caps from this period feature either an oilcloth or plastic sweat protector that covers the entire top panel. Note that air vents have remained a constant feature for all eras, and have changed little in style and construction.

R/N

Cap Body

1946-1956
The *Blue Cap* was used during this period and kept to the same configuration as the wartime version. The body and top was blue doeskin wool, with piping positioned around the crown. The Sides were padded and a removable stiffener was used. The body was

Lining from a 1990s Junior Officer's cap, fitted with a plastic oilskin styled sweat protector. The sweatband on this example is leather. Note the shape of the peak and rear positioned blackened air vents. *Private Collection.*

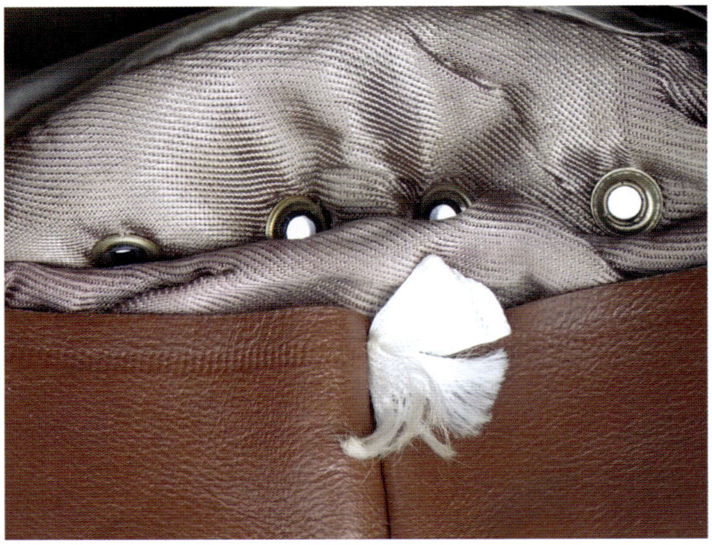

Lining and air vent backing detail of the 1990s cap. *Private Collection.*

In comparison to the more modern example the air vents on this 1970s cap are situated on each side. However, actual air vent style has barely altered. *Private Collection.*

A key Royal Navy Officer's cap example dating to April 1957, featuring the new regulation fixed vinyl top and chinstrap, introduced in 1956. The cap construction however remains consistent to wartime. Attributed to Lt.Cmdr. N.C. Atkinson RN. *Private Collection.*

stiffened by a double layer of hessian weave. In 1946 the white summer cotton top was re-approved, for use in home waters.

1956-1960s
In 1956 the *Blue Cap* was replaced by a version with a non-removable white vinyl top, which was similar in appearance to the cotton cover. The white top was to be used throughout the year in all regions. The vinyl top featured piping around its edge and tended to yellow.

1970s - Present
Most modern caps are of the frame construction. High-end Outfitters, such as Gieves & Hawkes Ltd. offer a white cotton top, while cheaper contract caps have either a fixed or removable white vinyl top. Some makers also offer a *Blue Cap* option, however these are less common.

The construction of the body is similar to that of wartime, with the hessian body stiffening and a blue body. Neither the top nor Sides are padded, giving the frame caps more of a lightweight appearance. The woven mohair band is also similar to that of wartime, measuring around 4cm in width.

Peak
For officers of Commander and above, the rank details worn on the peak is similar to that of wartime, although the relevant characteristics mentioned below apply, as for Junior officers.

1946-1956
As wartime. A patent leather peak topside and rim, with green skiver leather underside. Hardboard was also used to stiffen the peak.

1956-1960s
As above.

1970s - Present
In plan view, compared to wartime, the peak is "D" in shape and appears almost oversized. Peaks from high-end outfitters are patent leather with a vinyl rim and a skiver underside, while service caps, from the likes of Compton Webb (Headdress) Ltd., were vinyl.

A 1980s Royal Navy Officer's cap made by Compton Webb, missing its cap badge. The top is removable and made of ribbed white vinyl, which was used from 1956. *Private Collection.*

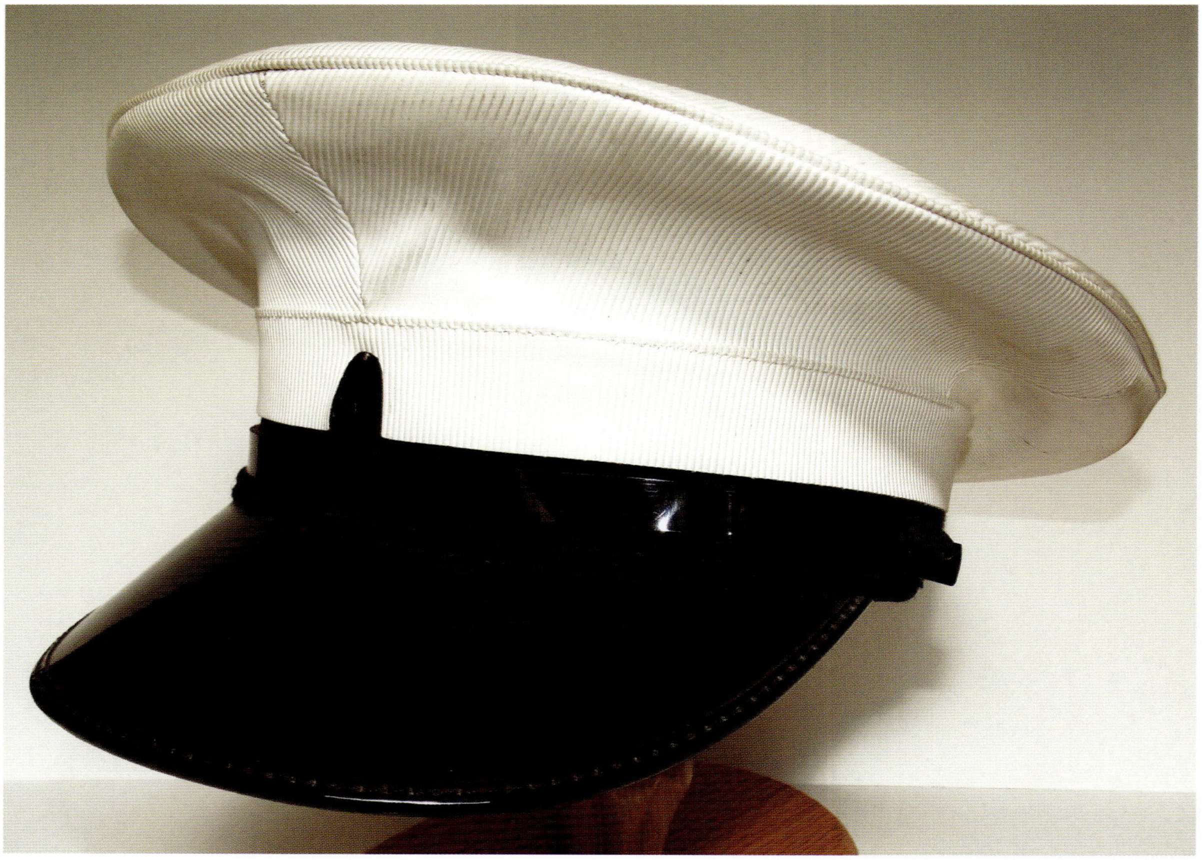

Detail of the Compton Webb vinyl cover. *Private Collection.*

1980s Junior R/N Officer's peak detail: Compton Webb.

Close-up detail of a vinyl R/N peak and rim. The peak is "D" shaped and appears oversized like a duck bill, which can be seen more clearly in the first photograph. *Private Collection.*

Cap Badge

The Royal Navy device on post-war caps is largely the same as those used during the Second World War, albeit with the change of crown pattern. The badge consists of a metal fouled anchor surrounded by embroidered gold laurel leaves, surmounted by an embroidered crown.

1946-1953
The Imperial crown of King George VI was used.

1953 - Present
In February of 1953, the Imperial crown was replaced by the St Edward's crown of Queen Elizabeth II. On the badge face, the cloth backing panel should have a minimum border of 5mm in width, while the entire device should be positioned centrally to match the front seam of the white top.

It is difficult to identify a St. Edward's crown to a particular post-war period, although early versions appear to have had a fuller velvet cap below the arches, while most modern crowns appear more *machine made* and balanced, with brighter looking gold/yellow wire.

An early Queen's Crown Royal Navy device from 1957. This style of this badge remains in current issue and has altered little, but most notably in the crown shape. Made by Griscti's Malta Embroiderers. *Private Collection.*

Chinstrap

1946-1960s
The chinstrap was that used during the war, being patent leather with blackened metal buckles. As is evident in the 1957 example, it would appear that black vinyl chinstraps were first used when the vinyl top was introduced, in 1956.

1970s - Present
The configuration of the chinstrap remained unchanged, although high-end tailored caps use blackened leather, which appears plasticised, compared to cheaper caps that use the black vinyl chinstrap with black plastic buckles and rivets.

Side Buttons

Royal Air Force and Royal Navy side buttons were identical in size and appearance, and as such shared the same characteristics post-war.

1946-1960s
Post-war side buttons of this period tended to be flat faced and covered in blue cloth to match the cap's body. The dimensions reflected those of wartime.

1970s - Present
More expensive cap makers use flat blue cloth covered side buttons, which appear finer looking than those of the war. Cheaper service caps use a black plastic button with a textured face to mimic the cotton surface.

Lining

1946-1956
The lining appeared as that used during the war, and tended not include the addition of a sweat protector or air vents, although in some cases details of the maker's label changed, as well as that of the Royal Warrant.

1956-1960s
As above, but usually with the addition of a semi-transparent oilskin sweat protector, covering the full top section of the lining.

1970s - Present
As more expensive caps are mostly of the frame pattern, the lining consists of the leather sweatband and body lining, while the underside of the cotton cover acts as the top lining element. A narrower sweat protector panel, running from the front to rear, connects to the body and cap crown stiffener, and provides a place for the maker's label.

Some cheaper contract caps have a dark bronze coloured lining and can be fitted with a clear acetate full top sweat protector, that yellows over time on early caps. The maker's label usually consists of a white paper label showing the NATO stock number. In most cases the sweatbands are imitation leather or brown vinyl.

Dating a Peak Cap

"How can I date a British Officer's peak cap to the Second World War?" or *"Is my cap authentic and original?"* These are perhaps the two most important questions that face a collector, and answering the one can often help answer the other.

When a cap has provenance then doubts to its authenticity should not be a major concern. If you are not so lucky and your cap is lacking in any helpful markings, noting the combination of relevant features highlighted in the Branch chapters should allow you to discover whether the cap is original or not.

If all the features appear consistent and you are certain that the cap has not been altered, modified or tampered with, then dating can be narrowed down to pre-1953. This is the earliest date that you can state with much certainty, unless mitigating circumstances exist.

Furthermore, uniforms tended to be ordered around the date of the Officer's commission, for a significant promotion or at the period of a major change in the dress regulations, such as that during the advent of HRH Queen Elizabeth II, where many Officers kept their wartime peak caps, changing only the badge and side buttons to the new Queen's Crown.

So which mitigating circumstances will allow you to date a cap more precisely? In this section I have shared some of the techniques that I have used successfully, however, with a little creative thinking I am sure many others exist.

Name, Rank and Serial Number

While most Officers chose to write their name(s), rank, initials or serial number somewhere in the cap lining, most usually on the

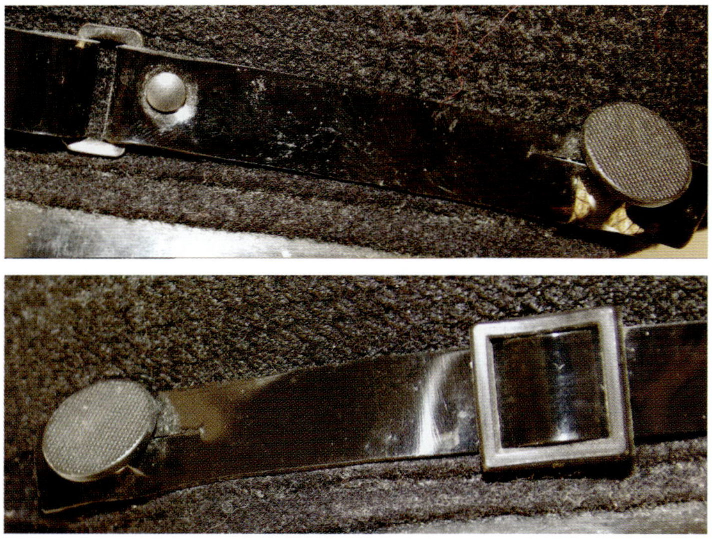

This post-war R/N chinstrap displays the same construction as wartime examples, although the buckles are a mix of plastic and blackened metal, while the strap itself is vinyl. Leather was also used by some Outfitters. Vinyl seemed the material of choice for contract peak caps from the 1970s onwards. *Private Collection.*

Another feature of contract caps are the plastic side buttons, made to the same dimensions and style as standard cloth covered variations. *Private Collection.*

Observe how the lining of this 1957 cap is nearly identical to wartime, save for the addition of an oilskin sweat-protector. Despite its poor condition it displays quite nicely the hessian body stiffener, as well as the hardboard peak stiffening, under the green leather skiver. *Private Collection.*

Lining from a 1980s R/N cap, typical of all contract caps. The sweatband is imitation leather while the maker's label is a simple white printed label, in this case from Compton Webb. *Private Collection.*

Close-up detail of a late post-war cap's body, showing the hessian stiffener, nylon lining and imitation leather sweatband. *Private Collection.*

leather sweatband, this was not a common practise implemented by all, interesting considering the number of serving Officers during that time. Often a quick research on a name can turn up details about the Officer's war service, which can be used to narrow down the cap's date to a specific year.

Bear in mind also that a cap with provenance or with researchable details written inside does not necessarily mean that it was the Officer's wartime cap. In some cases however where Officers were *Hostilities Only* or were retired soon after the war ended, the probability that the cap is wartime would be high.

Makers' Label

Studying the outfitters label can often prove fruitful, especially when there is the addition of a Royal Warrant together with, "By Appointment" or such similar.

In this situation, identifying the Royal Warrant to King George VI or Queen Elizabeth II can support the crown detail of the badge or serve to highlight the fact that the cap was made between 1937 and 1953, or indeed afterwards. Note also, a Royal Warrant with

Royal Cypher distinction

Royal Warrants

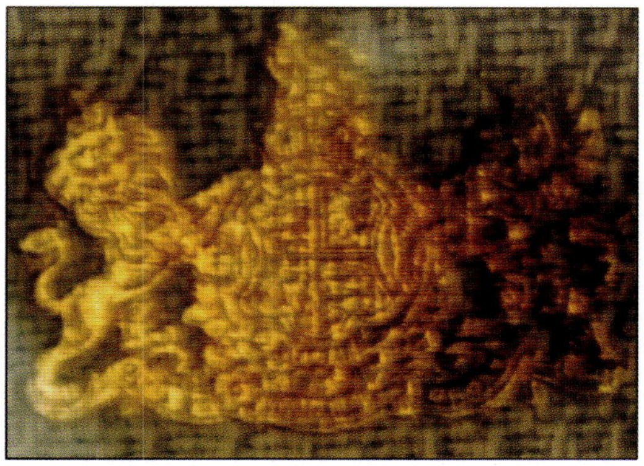

King George V
(1901 -1936).

King George VI
(1936 -1953).

Queen Elizabeth II
(1953 onwards).

A quick identification chart showing the relevant Royal Cyphers and Warrants.

"By Appointment to the Late King George VI" would suggest that the cap dates to around 1953.

Basic identification of contract made peak caps to the "modern" era can be done by using the maker's label, if we look at the font style of the text and the use of a contract number. Furthermore, the use of NATO Stock Numbers also gives us additional information, where the second set of digits denotes the country, which in the case of the United Kingdom is 99. It is thus worth noting that NSNs were introduced in 1975.

Grouping/Uniform Sets

If the cap came as part of a uniform set, either from the same Outfitter or it's rank insignia is consistent to the grouping, then the date given on the uniform makers' label can give a fair idea of the cap's age. Often main uniform items were ordered from a single Outfitter, who supplied many items of clothing even if they had to outsource. A specific example of this was the Outfitters Hector Powe, who offered caps made by Lincoln Bennett.

If you acquired a peak cap together with its original postal box, then looking carefully at the postage stamps and marks, as well as the Maker's details, can also give a good indication of the cap's age.

Study the Outfitters' Details

Peak caps made during the period of 1945 to 1953 and even during the latter part of that decade, changed little from those of wartime and are mostly indistinguishable. Luckily, with some Outfitters there are certain tell tale signs which we are given, or which are withheld, that can allow a cap to be dated to a particular period, such as address details, which could be a subject of research in itself.

Although not all Outfitters changed premises around key historical events, Gieves Ltd. is one of the exceptions, with Hawkes & Co. Ltd. being another.

If we focus first on Gieves Ltd. A wartime Gieves cap will show only *LONDON. W.1* as its address, although from 1920 to 1940 they were situated at *21 Old Bond Street.* Sometime during 1940, due to Luftwaffe bomb damage, the company relocated to Piccadilly. Examples of Gieves Ltd. cap labels can be seen in Chapter 9.

From 1946 until they joined with Hawkes & Co. Ltd. in 1974, where they assumed their current address of 1 Savile Row, Gieves Ltd were situated at *27 Old Bond Street. London.* Bear in mind that late-1950s caps may not show an address (as wartime labels), and tend to be square shaped, with a dominate Gieves Limited, not to be confused with a wartime label. Furthermore a Hawkes & Co.

An example of using the cap badge dating method. The cap badge on the left was used from the 1920s to 1970, when the WR regiment was amalgamated into the WFR. The right cap badge was redesigned and used from 1970 to 2007. *Private Collection.*

A typical label from a contract made R/N cap. The label states the cap's size, NATO Stock number (99 being the UK), company details and contract number. Other maker's may also list a construction date. It may also be possible to obtain the cap's date through researching a contract number. *Private Collection.*

Ltd. peak cap can be dated to post-1974 from the addition of the name Gieves to their labels.

Alkit Ltd. peak caps which display a white rectangular label marked with the address of *Cambridge Circus. London WC.2* can be dated from the 1920s, and include wartime. Sometime post-war the cap label became blue and triangular in shape, which is most commonly encountered on 1960s caps. Before and during the Second World War Alkit supplied all services of the military, although after the war this tended to mainly be RAF caps. Referring to the cap's material and crown can allow a more accurate date. An interesting point also, is that from 1941 to 1964 Alkit Ltd. held additional premises at *123 High Street Oxford. London.*

Herbert Johnson is a key Outfitter of post-war peak caps, supplying many of the regiments from the 1960s to the present day. However, certain of their peak caps can be dated to this post-war period from the addition of the "By Appointment to the Late King George VI," which would signify a date of 1953. Again this is dependent on the cap having its original World War II features, such as King's Crown device.

This illustration of a Royal Scots Dragoon Guards Dress cap, serves to show how regiment amalgamation can result in a new cap colour and style being issued. This particular cap design was used from 1971.

Regiment and Cap Badges

After the Second World War, and during the 1970s in particular, many regiments of the British Army were amalgamated together which had the effect of new badges and buttons being designed for the new regiments.

Before I go into this, I want to mention a relevant and important point for cap dating. Although specific to post-war Worcestershire Regiment cap badges, it may also be the case with other regiments. Whilst the elongated star badge remained unchanged from 1923 to 1970, during a period from 1958 to 1969 the badge of the Mercian Brigade was used on both Forage and Service caps. However, it seems this practise did not alter the side buttons which still featured the Worcestershire Regiment star.

Back to the main point, and if we take the Worcesters as an example, in 1970 the Worcestershire Regiment was amalgamated into the Worcestershire and Sherwood Foresters Regiment, which then became the 2nd Battalion, Mercian Regiment (Worcesters and Foresters), in 2007. This can allow us to place a date of a particular cap to a specific time frame, and together with other components it could be possible to narrow this date down further.

However, I must stress that this technique is only relevant to date a cap to before a certain significant date change, where it displays the old cap badge/buttons or colour scheme. As Officers serving through the changeover would have replaced the aforementioned details.

A more obvious example would be with that of the Royal Scots Dragoon Guards, which was formed from an amalgamation of the Royal Scots Greys and the 3rd Carabiniers, in 1971. The Forage cap took the vandyked band of the Royal Scots Greys and the yellow colour and piping of the 3rd Carabiniers, as well as combining their previous cap badges to create their current Forage cap. Whilst dating can easily be refined to pre or post-1971, this serves to highlight how a cap design or a colour change can affect the dating process.

Also by learning when a particular regiment of corps was formed can also help date a cap more precisely. If we take a KC cap badged to the REME, we can narrow down the date to between the end of 1942 and 1953. However there still remains the possibility that the Officer might have been transferred from another regiment or corps.

Also studying the design of the cap's badge can be a good indicator of age. In the case of the Army Dental Corps the wartime cap badge featured the intertwined abbreviation of ADC surrounded by a wreath and surmounted by the crown. The design was later changed to that of a dragon clutching a sword in his mouth, surrounded by a wreath and surmounted by the crown. The cap badge of the Royal Corps of Signals is also another good example.

The last part of this chapter should be used as a quick basic dating guide. However, for a more precise identification you must get your hands on the actual cap and refer additionally to the previous relevant chapters. Dig deeper into the cap's make-up; cross-examine each component and feature to discover if a more accurate date and authentication is possible.

Crowns

The very first step in identifying a cap should be a quick observation of the crown detail of badge, or side button if they display a crown.

Certain cap badge designs were changed after the Second World War, which can thus aid in dating a cap to a particular period, as was the case with the Royal Electrical and Mechanical Engineers.

This can give you an initial identification as to whether the cap is pre or post-1953. If the cap looks too new or shiny, then the chances are that badge has been wrongly added to the cap, which can often be the case with Online auctions.

First World War

British Officer's peak caps from around 1904 to the post-First World War period have varied styles depending on the branch. However, when compared to those of the 1930s and 1940s the differences are notable. Patent leather peaks tended to be shorter and thinner, with a rounded appearance, while chinstraps were narrow in width, at 0.9cm.

Lining material on early Forage caps was usually light coloured and featured a pale leather sweatband. Many examples also exhibit a drawstring mesh extension added to the sweatband, like the skullcap style found on cloth helmets or earlier Forage cap linings. Celluloid or oilskin were both used as a sweat-protector.

Army Service caps tended to use a metal stiffener to keep the shape of the top while the cap was usually stiffened with leather. These had a *Stiff* pattern look and in respect to its general construction and peak dimensions, conformed to World War II period caps. Royal Navy caps and Army Forage caps had less of a bevel or overhang to their Top, making the cap look stockier in style.

Army Service cap of Substantive Colonel and higher were either the Forage cap with a top cover or the Service Dress cap. The peak on the Service dress cap was patent leather with gold embroidered oak-leaf rank detailing. Observing the detail of the side button belonging to a Colonel's cap can also help in the dating process. Within the garter is the Royal Cypher, which for World War I was GvR.

Again, in some cases dating can be determined by looking at the makers' label. For example, a cap made by Hawkes & Co. Ltd. displaying the address of *14 Piccadilly* would date the cap to pre 1912, while a similar cap displaying the address of *1 Savile Row. W. Late 14 Piccadilly*, would date the cap firmly to within the First World War Period.

A brief note on pre-1901 Forage caps, which although not strictly relevant to aid our purposes of dating and identification, might prove interesting nevertheless.

Whatever the style of the Victorian Forage cap, a coloured or embroidered oak-leaf band was a predominant feature. Chinstraps on earlier caps were a thin strip of leather attached to the cap

The Royal Corps of Signals was another such example of using a cap badge to determined a peak cap's date.

lining, while the actual lining tended to be either red or blue in colour and quilted.

Forage caps from around the 1860s display a rectangular peak shape, resembling a French Kepi in style, while in the latter part of that era the peaks became distinctly round, smaller and more upright. The more recognisable peak cap style came into its own around 1900.

The highlighted side button is from an Army Forage cap that dates to 1900/1901. It is slightly larger in diameter than those used by 1914, and is made of bronze rather than gilt. The crown is that used by Queen Victoria, which was replaced in 1901.

Inter-war

During the Inter-war years up until the start of the Second World War, British Officers' peak caps underwent minor changes to the top shape and peak, although the narrow chinstrap remained constant. Perhaps the change in style occurred during the early 1920s when the shape of the Royal Navy cap top was widened.

Wartime and Post-war

During the Second World War the chinstrap width was widened and by the end of the conflict the *Soft* cap pattern had taken preference, which we can associate with both post-war Service and Dress caps. Army Service caps used by Officers of Substantive Colonel and higher no longer displayed oak-leaf detailing on a patent peak, but instead used the standard cloth covered peak as used by all other Officers.

For identification of the various side button materials used, please refer to the corresponding chart. Whilst plastic and Stay-bright were the materials of choice post-war, it must be noted that gilt is still used by Senior Officers. White metal is used by Lord Lieutenants and the like, with blackhorn being used by the Rifle Brigade. An example of a blackhorn button can be seen in Chapter 4.

Post-war, from 1956 white vinyl was used for the top of Royal Navy Officer's peak caps and during the 1970s vinyl and plastic was used for "patent" peaks, chinstraps and side buttons. Stay-bright was also used for Army caps buttons from the 1950s. Around the 1970s, Frame caps were used by the Royal Navy and remain so to this day.

From the 1960s the shape of Royal Air Force and Army cap cloth covered peaks became shorter and more rounded than those of wartime and immediately after, while R/N peaks tend to be

RAF Cap Badges
(Not to scale).

Pre 1953 (Wartime).

Post 1953.

A quick identification chart highlighting the differences between a wartime Junior RAF Officer's cap badge, and that of post-war. The most obvious being the crown differences.

Navy Cap Badges
(Not to scale).

Pre 1953 (Wartime).

Post 1953.

This quick identification chart highlights the differences between a wartime Royal Navy Officer's cap badge, and that of post-war.

Army Cap Badges
(Not to scale).

Pre 1953 (Wartime).

Post 1953.

Whilst listing a complete pictorial comparison between wartime and post-war metal or embroidered army cap badges would no doubt be useful, it is regrettably impossible. However, the two Substantive Colonel's cap badge examples can be used as a quick reference.

Side profile view of a World War I era Army Forage cap. Note the thin short peak and narrow chinstrap, typical features of such early and inter-war caps. By the start of World War II the peak shape had enlarged, while the chinstrap width changed soon after. *Private Collection.*

Lining from a World War I Forage cap. Note the shape and size of the peak, as well as the pale leather sweatband with drawstring adjustment. The latter a feature that was phased out by the end of the Second World War. The sweat protector is celluloid. *Private Collection.*

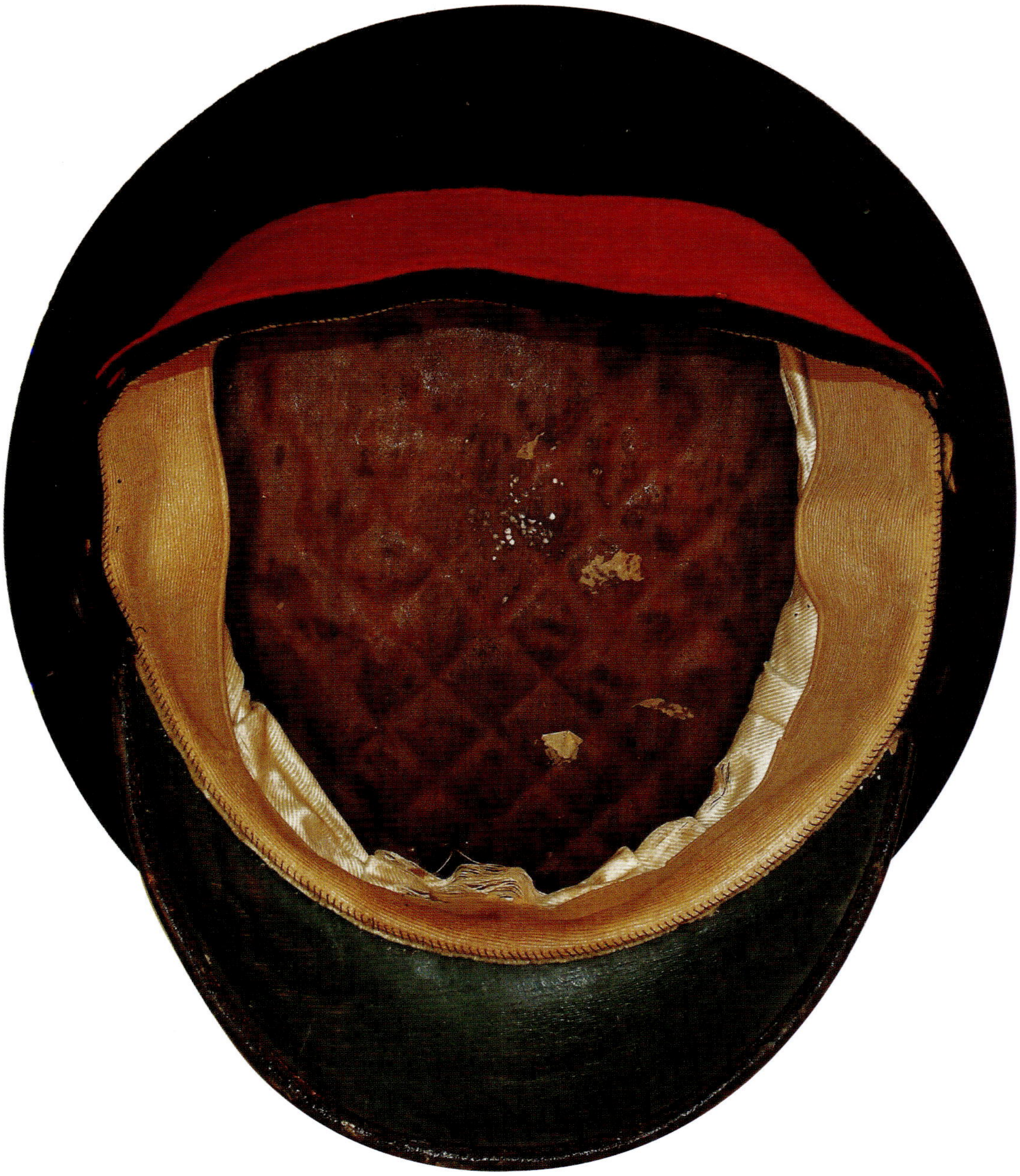

Lining from a World War I era Deputy Lieutenant's Forage cap, exhibiting similar features to the Army Forage cap. Note however the different lining style, which is padded and covered in orange oilskin. *Private Collection.*

A World War I Staff Officer's gilt side button. This button is the same as that used by Substantive Colonels and Brigadiers. *Private Collection.*

This quick identification chart displays the various materials used for peak cap side buttons, regardless of branch and period. Note the blackened metal Australian Military Forces button, mentioned in Chapter 7.

A bronze side button from a 1900s Victorian era Army Forage cap. The button is slightly larger than later side buttons. Note also the crown shape, which was used until 1901. *Private Collection.*

oversized, with a vinyl rim. The cap style of later post-war RAF and Army caps tend to be of the saddle shape.

However, unless a cap was acquired first hand from the Officer that wore it, we will never truly know the path our caps took to our display cabinets, and what this journey involved. However, it is by studying the features and comparing that we can see if something looks right, or whether it has been tampered with.

So to summarise this dating information into a quick, broad and basic overview;

A peak cap which has a KC badge, cloth body, peak and top, a (patent) leather chinstrap, peak and rim, with either brass, gilt or cloth covered side buttons, denotes *Wartime.*

A peak cap which has QC badge, cloth body (with or without a vinyl top), vinyl chinstrap, peak and rim, with either Stay-bright or plastic side buttons, denotes *Post-war.*

Living History, Re-enactment and Reproduction

How to spot a fake? Luckily, compared to other areas of Second World War headdress, British peak caps tend not to be forged and when so are relatively easy to spot. However, there is no doubt that as the prices are steadily increasing this will become a more important issue to become aware of.

There are a number of companies catering to Living History and re-enactment communities, not to mention such events as the Goodwood Revival, which also supply current issue military insignia and badges. The vast majority of wartime caps that we encounter today appear used, worn, faded or otherwise, and we must take into consideration that during their heyday they would have appeared new and spotless, making these modern copies ideally suited for their purpose.

Original RAF Officer's device compared to a modern reproduction.

Original R/N Officer's device compared to a modern reproduction.

There are a variety of modern embroidered RAF and R/N Officer's cap badges available on the market, (not to mention Army badges), made to a similar configuration and dimension as wartime originals. However, when compared to originals the differences are obvious.

Modern badges tend to be used on post war or reproduction caps. However, it is not unheard of for some to be used on older or original caps and be passed off as original period pieces. Although, not as common as their Third Reich counterparts, these tend to be focused on more desirable and rarer pieces, such as an RAF Chaplain's peak cap.

The differences between original wartime issue and various modern badge examples can be seen in the photos. Modern copies appear "machine" made and more "uniform" than those of wartime, while the colours and materials used look brighter and have a yellow hue. Some copies are evidently of a higher quality than others, but focusing on the crown detail can serve to highlight any differences in respect to an original.

CHAPTER NINE

Outfitters

This chapter lists the majority of known Outfitters who supplied His Majesty's military Officers with peak caps, during and prior to the Second World War, as well as a list of post-war Outfitters, some of which are still trading.

As most Outfitters were not exclusive to a particular service, they have been presented in alphabetical order to allow quick referencing. However, I have added a note to show which branches an Outfitter is known to have supplied. It might be the case that cap examples exist from a specific Outfitter to a particular branch which is not listed below.

Disclaimer: Due to the nature of collecting and the absence of an official list of Military Outfitters, the number of wartime suppliers cannot be taken as definitive. Also the inclusion of illustrations are for identification purposes only.

A.J. White Ltd. Hatters & Cap Makers.
Burlington Gardens. [London] W.1.
Supplied: Army.
(England).

A & L. Corne. Hat & Cap Makers.
Shorts Gardens.
London. W.C.2.
Supplied: Army.
(England).

A & W Lambert.
Edinburgh.
Supplied:
(Scotland).

Aldertons
The Strand, London.
Supplied: Army.
(England).

Alkit Ltd., Naval Military R.A.F and Sporting Outfitters.
Cambridge Circus. London, W.C.2. (Square label).
123 High Street, Oxford. (1941-1964).
Supplied: Mainly RAF
(England).

Aucott Military Tailors.
Sackville Street. W.1.
Supplied: Army.
(England).

Army & Navy Cooperative Society Limited.
London.
Supplied: Army. Royal Navy.
(England).

Asquith & Lord Ltd.
Bombay.
Supplied: RAF.
(India).

Austin Reed.
Regent Street. W.1. London.
Supplied: Army, Royal Air Force & Royal Navy.
(England).

Ayres & Smith.
London. W.
For: Strong Bros Tailors & Outfitters. Moreton-in-Marsh.
Supplied: Royal Air Force. Army.
(England).

Bates Hatter.
21. Jermyn Street. St. James London.
Supplied: Mainly Royal Air Force. (Not R/N).
(England).

Battersby.
London.
Supplied: Army, Royal Air Force.
(England).

Bright & McIvor.
Calcutta.
Supplied: Army.
(India).

Burberrys Ltd.
Haymarket. London. S.W.1.
Supplied: Army, Royal Air Force.
(England).

Cater & Co.
56 Pall Mall. London. S.W.
Supplied: Army.
(England).

Chas. Hill & Sons Ltd. Hat & Cap Manufacturers.
238 Lambton Quay. Wellington.
Supplied: RAAF.
(Australia).

Christies.
London.
Sydney.
Supplied: RAF & Army.
(England).

Conway Williams.
Mayfair, London W.1 and Camberley.
Supplied: Army.
(England).

Dewbury & Son. Military Tailors & Outfitters.
86 Newgate St, London E.C.1.
Supplied: Army.
(England).

E. Parson
Rawalpindi
Supplied: Army.
(India).

Edward Smith.
25 Cork Street. Bond Street. London.
Supplied: Army.
(England).

E.W. Vero & Co.
London.
Supplied: Royal Air Force.
(England).

Finnigans Ltd.
Deansgate, Manchester.
Supplied: Army.
(England).

Flights Ltd. Military Tailors & Outfitters (until 1950).
New Burlington Street. London. W.1.
Aldershot. Camberley.
Supplied: RAF & Army.
(England).

G.A. Dunn & Co. Ltd.
373 - 4-5 Strand. Piccadilly Circus, 54-56 Oxford Street. London.
Supplied: Army.
(England).

Gardiner Ltd.
London.
Supplied: Royal Navy.
(England).

Gieves Ltd.
21 Old Bond Street. London. (Pre-1940).
80 Piccadilly. London. W.1. (1940-1946). Label marked London. W.1.
Supplied: Mainly Royal Navy.
(England).

Hamilton Uniform & Cap Company Ltd.
214-218 King William St.
Hamilton.
Supplied: RCN.
(Canada).

Harold H. Spence.
14 Silver Street. Kettering.
Supplied: RAF.
(England).

Harris & Reed Ltd.
29 Panton Street. Haymarket. London. S.W.
Supplied: Army.
(England).

Harry Hall Ltd. Naval – R.A.F. and Military Tailors.
181 Oxford Street, W.1
149 Cheapside. E.C.2
Supplied: Army.
(England).

Hawkes & Co. Ltd.
1 Savile Row. W. (1912-1974).
Supplied: Army. RAF.
(England).

Hector Powe.
165 Regent Street. London. W.1.
Supplied: Army. Royal Air Force. Royal Navy.
(England).

Henry Morgan & Co. Hatters.
Colonial House, Montreal.
Supplied: RCAF.
(Canada).

ALKIT LTD. (PRE 1941).

ALKIT LTD. (MIDWAR).

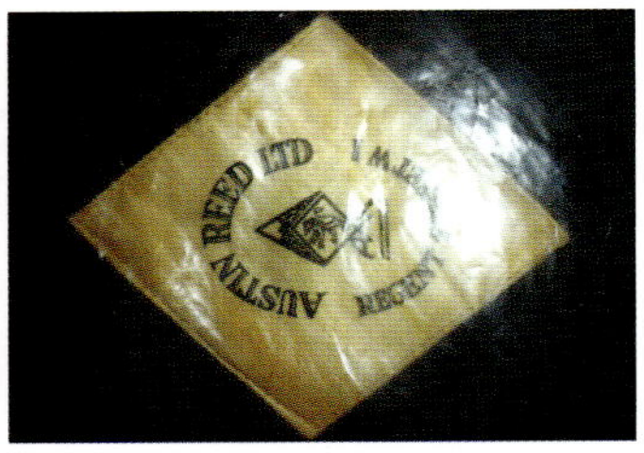

AUSTIN REED LTD.

BATES HATTER (SWEATBAND AND LINING).

BATTERSBY.

CATER & CO.

E. W. VERO & CO.

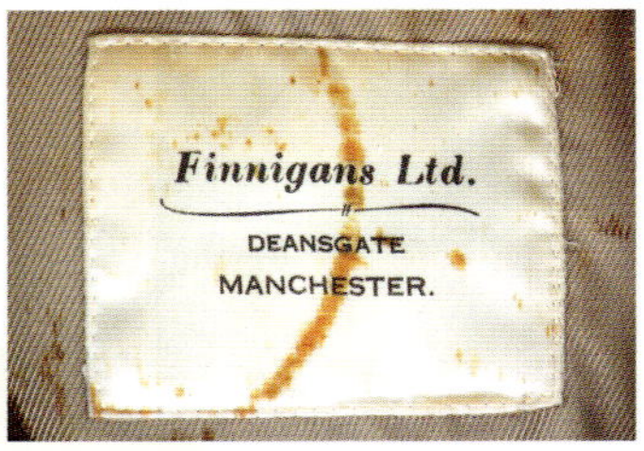

FINNIGANS LTD.

FLIGHTS LTD.

G.A.DUNN & CO.

GIEVES LTD. (ARMY PRE 1939).

GIEVES LTD.

HAMILTON UNIFORM & CAP COMPANY LTD.

HARRY HALL LTD.

HAWKES & CO LTD.

HECTOR POWE

HENRY MORGAN & CO HATTERS.

HORNE BROTHERS.

H. RUMSBY WELLS.

J. B. JOHNSTONE LTD.

J. DANIELS & CO.

Examples of Outfitter's labels found in wartime peak caps. Note that the font and style of the illustrations may vary slightly. *G.A. Dunn & Co. label courtesy of James Katzenstein.*

A 1939 dated Hawkes & Co. Ltd. advertisement, as found in period military magazines and journals. *Courtesy of Gieves & Hawkes.*

Herbert Chappell
58 Conduit Street. W.1.
50 Gresham Street. E.C.2.
Supplied: Royal Air Force.
(England).

Herbert Johnson (Bond Street) Ltd.
38 New Bond Street. London. W.
Supplied: Army & RAF.
(England).

H.J. Nicoll & Co. Outfitters.
Regent St, London. W.
Supplied: Royal Air Force. (Same style logo as Bates Hatter).
(England).

Hobson & Sons. London Ltd. Naval Military & Civil Tailors.
London and Camberley.
Lexington Street London .
Supplied: Royal Navy & Army.
(England).

Hope Brothers Ltd.
84-86 Regent Street. London. W.
And Provinces.
Supplied: Army.
(England).

Horne Brothers.
Oxford Street.W.1.
Supplied: Army, Royal Navy. Royal Air Force.
(England).

H. Rumsby Wells. Ladies & Gentlemen's Cap Makers.
Norwich.
For: Moss Bros & Co. Ltd. Covent Garden. W.C.2.
Supplied: Army.
(England).

J. Bidencope & Son
Murray Street, Hobart, Tasmania.
Supplied: Australian Army.
(Australia).

J. Compton Sons & Webb Ltd.
London.
Supplied: Army.
(England).

James Forsyth Ltd.
St. Albans.
Supplied: Royal Navy.
(England).

J.B. Johnstone Ltd.
34 & 5, Sackville St. London. W. & Dublin.
Supplied: Army.
(England)

J. Daniels & Co. Military Tailor & Outfitters.
1. Artillery Place. Woolwich. & 34, Bury Street. St. James's, S.W.
39. Conduct Street. London. W.1.
Supplied: Army.
(England).

J. Lan. Clan Luxury Caps.
Canada.
Supplied: RCAF.
(Canada).

J.M. Clément.
Quebec.
Supplied: Army.
(Canada).

J.R. Stephens & Co. Ltd.
Nairobi.
Supplied: Army.
(Kenya).

Jones, Chalk & Dawson.
6 Sackville Street. London. W.
Supplied: Army.
(England).

J.S. Wilson Limited.
London. W.
For: A. B. Cheese. 324 High Street. Lincoln.
Supplied: Royal Air Force.
(England).

Lock & Co. Hatters.
St. James's Street. London.
Supplied: Army. (Same style logo as Bates Hatter).
(England).

Lincoln Bennett & Co.
Burlington Gardens. Old Bond Street. London.
Howe.
Supplied: Royal Navy.
(England).

L Silberston & Sons Ltd.
London.
Supplied: Army.
(England).

M. Grant & Sons. Ltd.
London.
Supplied: Royal Navy.
(England).

Miller Rayner & Haysom Limited.
London. Southampton. Tilbury Dock. Liverpool.
Supplied: Royal Navy.
(England).

Monnery's Ltd. Outfitters.
London. Southampton. Liverpool.
Supplied: Royal Navy.
(England).

Moss Bros & Co. Ltd.
20-21 Kings Street. Covent Garden. London W.C.2.
Supplied: RAF & Army.
(England).

M.M. Shariff. High Class Hatters.
41. Moore Market. Madras.
Supplied: Army.
(India).

M. TX
Supplied: RAAF.
(Australia).

Muir Cap & Regalia Limited.
51 Simcoe Street. Toronto. Canada.
Supplied: Royal Canadian Air Force.
(Canada).

Peapes.
Sydney.
Supplied: Army.
(Australia).

Principal Cap/Uniform Cap.
Montreal. Canada.
Supplied: RCAF.
(Canada).

Rankin & Co. Ltd.
139 George Street, Hanover Square. London. W.
Calcutta, Simla, Lahore & Rawal Pindi.
Supplied: Army.
(India).

R.E. City. Service & Civilian Outfitters.
London & Branches.
Supplied: RAF.
(England).

R.W. Forsyth Ltd, Hatters.
Renfield Street, Glasgow & Edinburgh.
Supplied: Army.
(Scotland).

Sanders & Brightman of Luton.
Luton.
Supplied: Mainly Royal Navy. (& Army).
(England).

S.A.P.H.I.
Pretoria.
Supplied: Army, SAAF.
(South Africa).

J. DANIELS & CO. (SWEATBAND).

LINCOLN BENNETT & CO.

LINCOLN BENNETT (SWEATBAND).

L. SILBERSTON & SONS LTD.

M. GRANT & SONS. LTD.

MONNERY'S LTD OUTFITTERS.

MOSS BROS & CO. LTD

MOSS BROS & CO. LTD

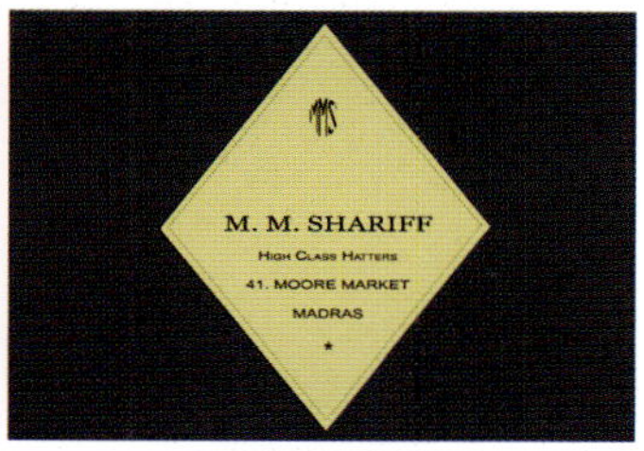

M. M. SHARIFF.

M. TEX.

PRINCIPAL CAP.

SANDERS & BRIGHTMAN.

SIMPSON.

SIMPSON & SON.

SINCLAIR & THOMAS.

STOKES CAP & REGALIA LTD.

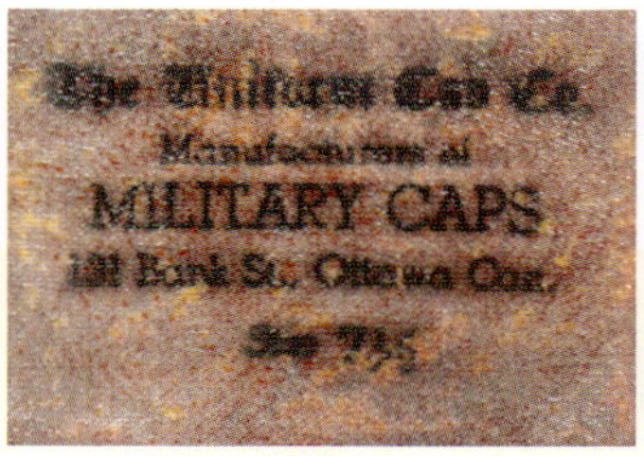

THE UNIFORM CAP CO.

THRESHER & GLERRY OUTFITTER.

THOMAS & STONE.

VAISH BROS.

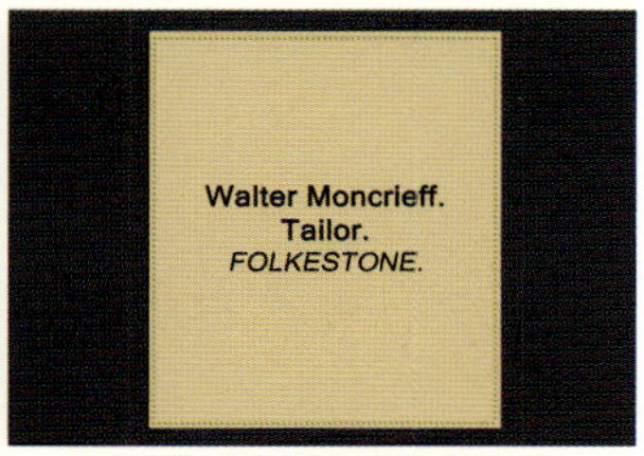

WALTER MONCRIEFF TAILOR.

Additional examples of Outfitter's labels found in wartime peak caps. Note that the font and style of the illustrated examples may vary slightly. *J. Daniels & Co. label courtesy of James Katzenstein. Lincoln Bennett & Co., M.TX, Principal Cap, and Stokes Cap & Regalia Limited, courtesy of Tod Rathbone. Rathbone Museum of World War II Aviators.*

Scott & Co.
1 Old Bond Street. Piccadilly. W.
Supplied: Mainly Army (& R/N from Gieves Ltd.).
(England).

Simpson.
Piccadilly, London. W.1.
Supplied: Royal Air Force.
(England).

Simpson & Son.
63 South Audley Street. London W.1.
Supplied: Royal Air Force & Army.
(England).

Sinclair & Thomas.
West Nile Street. Glasgow.
Supplied: Army.
(Scotland).

S. Sesti.
Cairo.
Supplied: Army.
(Egypt).

Stokes Cap & Regalia Limited.
93 Church Street. Toronto.
Supplied: RCAF.
(Canada).

S.W. Silver & Co.
London. Portsmouth. Southampton. Liverpool & Howe.
Supplied: Royal Navy.
(England).

The Aldershot Stores. Cap Makers.
Aldershot.
Supplied: Army.
(England).

The Standard. Harvey's Outfitters.
73 Leadenhall Street. London. E.C.3.
Tel Avenue 3340.
Supplied: Royal Navy.
(England).

The Uniform Cap Co. Manufacturers of Military Caps.
131 Bank St. Ottawa. Canada.
Supplied: RCAF.
(Canada).

Thresher & Glerry Outfitter.
152. Strand. London.
Supplied: Army.
(England).

Thomas & Stone. Hat & Cap Makers.
108 Jerymn Street. St James's, London. S.W.1.
Supplied: Army.
(England).

Tress & Co. London.
G.E. Carrington.
53, High Street, Old Brompton,
Carlton House, Regent Street. S.W.
Supplied: Army.
(England).

Uniquip. Uniform Clothing & Equipment Co.
London E.C.1.
Supplied: Army.
(England).

Vaish Bros.
New Delhi.
Supplied: Royal Air Force.
(India).

Victor Jay and Company Ltd.
London.
Supplied: Royal Air Force.
(England).

Walter Bernard & Sons Ltd.
97 Jermyn Street. St. James London.
Supplied: Army.
(England).

Walter Moncrieff Tailor.
Folkstone
Supplied: Royal Air Force.
(England).

William Scully Limited.
Montreal.
Supplied: Royal Canadian Navy.
(Canada).

Wm Anderson & Son Ltd. Military Outfitters.
Edinburgh & Glasgow.
Supplied: Army.
(Scotland).

Woodrow.
18, Donegal Place, Belfast.
46 Piccadilly. London. W.
Manchester, Liverpool, Glasgow & Dublin.
Supplied: Army.
(England).

W. Wood & Sons Ltd. Tailors & Outfitters.
North & South Shields.
Supplied: Royal Navy. Merchant Navy.
(England).

The following lists a number of suppliers who are known to have made badges and accessories for 1936-1945 era peak caps.

Alkit Ltd.
London.
Supplied: Metal badges.
(England).

FIRMIN & SONS. LTD.

FIRMIN & SONS. LTD.

J. R. GAUNT & SONS LTD.

GEORGE KENNING & SON LTD.

MUIR CAP & REGALIA LIMITED.

STEPHEN SIMPSON.

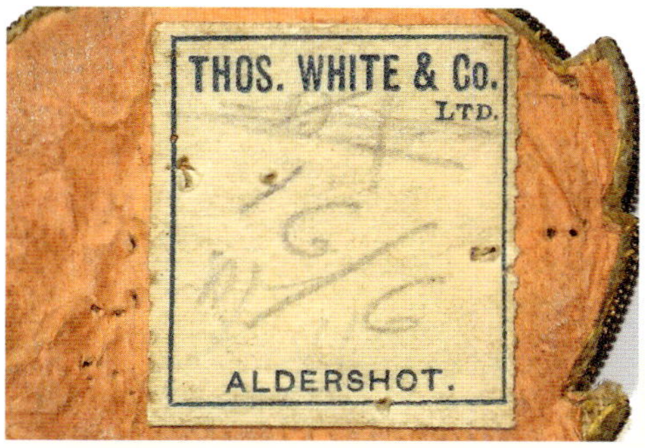

THOMAS WHITE & SONS LTD.

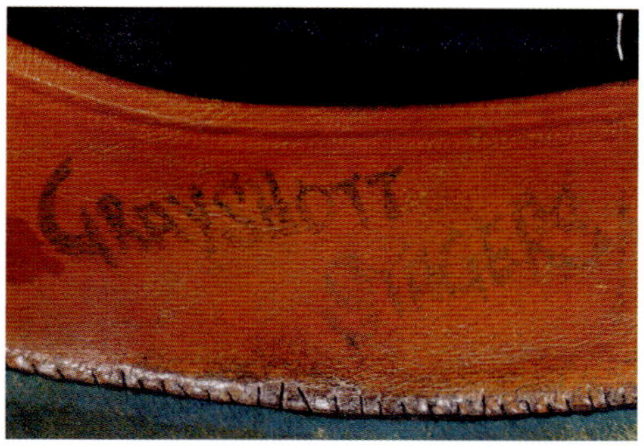

GRAYSHOTT STAGERS.

Examples of Outfitter's labels found on wartime cap badges, and sweatband. Note that the font and style of the illustrated examples may vary slightly, and as with the other sets, have been included for purposes of identification.

Firmin & Sons.
8 Cork Street. London. W.1.
Supplied: All branches, metal or embroidered badges.
(England).

J.R. Gaunt & Son Ltd.
London
Supplied: All branches, metal or embroidered badges
(England).

George (Geo) Kenning & Son Ltd. Goldsmiths - Masonic Depot.
Eagle Wharf Road. London. N.1.
Date: Until 1956.
Supplied: Royal Navy device.
(England).

Muir Cap & Regalia Limited.
51 Simcoe Street. Toronto. Canada.
Supplied: RCAF device.
(Canada).

Stephen Simpson. Gold & Silver Lace, Manufacturer and Embroiderer.
Avenham Road Works, Preston.
Supplied: Royal Navy device.
(England).

Thomas White & Son. Ltd.
Aldershot.
Supplied: Senior Officer's cap devices.
(England).

William Scully Limited.
Montreal.
Supplied: RCAF, RCAN devices.
(Canada).

Grayshott Stagers.
Supplied: Real Roan leather sweatbands.

The following list displays Outfitters who supplied post-war era caps and badges. Where possible I have added a date or period, however this does not necessarily imply that a company ceased trading, but rather it serves to highlight the fact that caps exist dating to that time period.

A. Grantham Ltd.
Supplied: Army, Royal Air Force & Royal Navy.
Dates: 1990s.
(England).

Alkit Ltd.
Cambridge Circus. London, W.C.2. (Triangle label).
123 High Street, Oxford. (Pre-1964).
Supplied: Mainly RAF.
Date: Pre-1990.
(England).

Ammo & Co. Ltd.
Supplied: Army
Date: 2000s to current.
(England).

Army & Navy Hat & Cap Co. Ltd. also **A & N Hat & Cap Co. Ltd.**
Supplied: R/N.
Date: Pre-1970s
(England).

Au Wai Lam & Co. Station Tailor.
RAF Kai Tak Hong Kong.
Supplied: RAF.
Date: 1960s.
(Hong Kong).

Bates Hatter.
Supplied: RAF.
Date: pre mid-2000s.
(England).

Bernard Weatherill Ltd. Military Tailors.
66 Conduit Street. London. W.1.
Supplied: Army.
Date: 1950s.
(England).

Cardinal Hat Co. Ltd.
50-52 Peckham Rye, London Se 15 4JR.
Supplied: Royal Air Force.
Date: 1970s.
(England).

Chan Tuck & Co.
Tailors & Outfitters Hong Kong
Supplied: Royal Air Force.
Date: 1970s.
(Hong Kong).

Compton Webb (Headdress) Ltd.
54 Newland. Witney. Oxon
Supplied: R/N.
Date: 1970s/1980s.
(England).

E.C. Snaith & Son Ltd.
20 Vale Street. Denbigh, Clwyd LL16 3BE
Supplied: Army. Royal Air Force. Royal Navy.
Date: Till present.
(England).

Flights Ltd.
Supplied: Army.
(England).

Foster & Foster Ltd.
London S.W.1.
Supplied: Royal Navy.
(England).

Gieves Ltd.
27 Old Bond Street. London. W.1.
Supplied: Mainly R/N.
Date: Pre 1974.
(England).

Gieves & Hawkes.
No.1 Savile Row. London.
Supplied: All branches.
Date: 1974 to present.
(England).

H. Berwald & Co.
London.
Supplied: Army.
Date: 1960s.
(England).

Hawkes & Co. Ltd.
1 Savile Row. London.
Supplied: Army.
Date: Pre-1974.
(England).

Herbert Johnson (Bond Street) Ltd.
38 New Bond Street. London. W.
13 Old Burlington Street. London W.1. (2007)
30 New Bond Street. London. W.1. (2000s)
25 Blenheim Avenue Fakenham, (2012)
Supplied; All Branches but mainly Army.
Date: To present.
(England).

A. GRANTHAM LTD.

ALKIT LTD. (1960s).

AU WAI LAM & CO. (1970s).

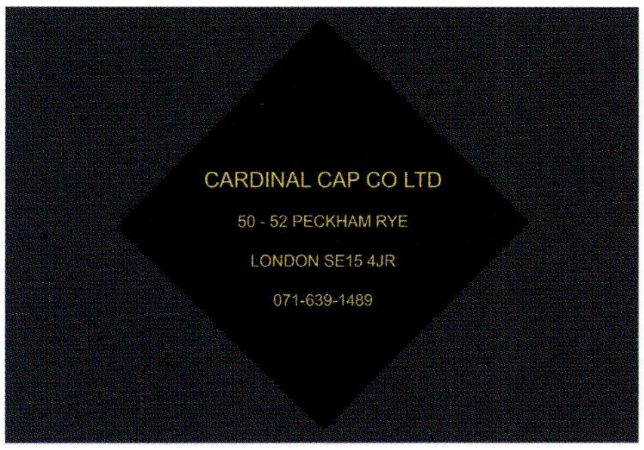

CARDINAL HAT CO. LTD.

COMPTON WEBB LTD.(1980s).

GIEVES LTD. (1946 - 1974).

GIEVES LTD.(1957 WITHOUT ADDRESS).

HERBERT JOHNSON LTD. (1960s).

HERBERT JOHNSON LTD. (DRESS).

HERBERT JOHNSON LTD. (2000s).

MOSS BROTHERS.

WILLIAM SCULLY LTD.

Examples of post-war Outfitter's labels. Note that the font and style of the illustrations may vary slightly. *Moss Brothers label courtesy of Courtesy of Tod Rathbone. Rathbone Museum of World War II Aviators.*

Hobson & Sons (London) Ltd.
Kenneth Road, Thundersley. Essex.
Supplied: R/N, RAF & Army.
Date: To present.
(England).

Horne Brothers Ltd.
London.
Supplied: RAF.
Date: 1950s.
(England).

Lock & Co. Hatters.
6 St. James's Street. London.
Supplied: Army.
(England).

Moss Brothers
Supplied: RAF & Army.
(England).

Patey (London) Ltd.
9 Gowlett Road, London. SE.
35 Connaught Street. London. W2.
Supplied: RAF & Army
Date: To present.
(England).

R.E. City Ltd. Tailors & Outfitters to the RAF.
Melcombe Street. London N.W.1.
Supplied: RAF.
(England).

Rifles Direct.
RHQ The Rifles. Peninsula Barracks, Romsey Road, Winchester.
Supplied: Rifle Regiments only.
Date: 2006 - Present.
(England).

Sanders & Brightman
Luton.
Supplied: Royal Navy. Army.
(England).

The Eastern Mfg. Co.
Bangalore City.
Supplied: Army
Date: 1950s.

Thomas & Stone. Hat & Cap Makers.
108 Jerymn Street. St James's, London. S.W.1.
Supplied: Army.
Date: Pre-1970s.
(England).

Toye Kenning & Spencer
Newtown Road. Bedworth. Warwickshire
Supplied: Army, RAF & Royal Navy.
Date: Till Present.
(England).

Weston Cap
Supplied: Army.
Date: Present.
(England).

William Jardine & Sons Ltd.
12-14 Forth Street. Edinburgh.
Supplied: Army.
Date: Pre 1980.
(Scotland).

Whilst many companies supplied post-war peak caps with metal or embroidered badges and insignia, I have only chosen to list those particularly relevant to this book.

E.C. Snaith & Son Ltd.
20 Vale Street. Denbigh, Clwyd LL16 3BE
Supplied: Army. Royal Air Force. Royal Navy.
Date: Till present.
(England).

Firmin & Sons Ltd.
Firmin House. 82-86 New Town Row. Birmingham
Supplied: All services.
Date: Till present.
(England).

Griscti's Malta Embroiderers.
Supplied: Royal Navy.
Date: 1950s

J.R. Gaunt Ltd.
Birmingham.
Supplied: All services.
Date: Till 1973.
(England).

Stephen Simpson. Gold & Silver Lace, Manufacturer and Embroiderer.
Avenham Road Works, Preston.
Supplied: Royal Navy device.
Date: Till 1991.
(England).

Toye Kenning & Spencer (Incorporating George Kenning & Spencer in 1956).
77 Warstone Lane. Birmingham.
Supplied: Army. Royal Air Force. Royal Navy.
Date: Till present.
(England)

CHAPTER TEN

Researching & Price Guide

Researching

Researching a peak cap, or indeed any item in your collection, is a good way to gain understanding of that particular item, and the person who wore it. Where and how it was used and by whom can often add to its value, but most importantly may provide a better idea of its age. However, researching British Second World war service records or Officers' names can often prove fruitless, that is unless you are a family member.

However, all is not lost! The internet is a great resource and can be used to help us, provided that your cap has either one or more of the following details: the Officer's full name, initials, serial number or branch. Using this information creatively can turn up results.

If we take a Royal Navy Officer's peak cap as an example. The cap has the name *Lt. J.B. Brown RNVR* written onto the sweatband. Searching this information in its entirety might not turn up any results, or worse still too many irrelevant results. However using a little creatively can prove very fruitful.

Searching for *Lt. Brown RNVR* might again turn up too many results. *Lt. J.B Brown* might be better but you will have to search through many records until you come to an officer of the Royal Navy. Trying different variations and matching them to the branch and initials can be successful. Also guessing a first name is a useful tip. We could try *Lt. John Brown* or *Lt James Brown* and so on. With a serial number this search can become more accurate.

This is not a guaranteed method of success as some Officers do not show up on any records, or in the case of a surname and Branch, such as *Stevens RNVR,* the result would be difficult to refine due to the number of Officers named Stevens of that particular branch.

Where can we use this information?

My personal favourite and first port of call when researching is *The London Gazette*. *The London Gazette* is not only a great tool for researching Officers of the Second World War, but provides a wealth of research on other historical periods and events, such as the First World War.

www.london-gazette.co.uk/search

The website gives the dates of awards, promotions and retirements, showing an Officer's name or initials, and serial number. Although not all Officers are listed, when a search is successful a wealth of information can be obtained.

To use this website is relatively straightforward. On the homepage you must use the advanced search function. First choose the historical event, in this case World War II. If you have any particular dates then you can fill out the appropriate date drop boxes, although I find it is much better to skip this section and simply fill out the Words entry box, "With the exact phrase."

This should produce some results, but to refine the search try using the various naming techniques I have given above. Try also selecting or de-selecting certain options of the advanced search. You will soon find what works best.

One of the first places to look should be an internet search engine. Type in the Veteran's name using "", for example, "*J.B. Brown.*" Depending on the results, try the techniques mentioned. This research option can be hit or miss, however I have had some surprising results.

A very useful website for our purposes, and one particularly interesting in its own right is, *World War II Unit Histories and Officers*. This website lists a large amount of Officers names and service record information from a selection of countries. Laid out by service branch, Officer's names are presented in alphabetical order. The British section is most impressive.

www.unithistories.com

Furthermore, important resources should you have access to them, are Army, Royal Navy and Air Force lists, detailing names, seniority and appointments. This wealth of information can allow more accurate dating. If we take a R/N Commander's peak cap as an example. The Officer was promoted to Commander in 1944, which would allow us to date the cap quite nicely.

Searching the War Graves registries or war memorials can also shed some light on an Officer, such as his service number, rank, family information or area that he came from. This option can be used to provide additional information or when no other avenue produces results.

Often research obtained from one method can uncover a new approach which can be used to continue the research in another. For example some time ago I acquired a RAF cap attributed to an Officer and although I was given some information about his service, it was after conducting an internet search that lead me to a U-boat website, detailing this Officer's last sortie, aircraft number and crew.

There are no doubt other options for researching an Officer's military background or fate, but these can be difficult when there is no family connection, or consent in obtaining a service record. The techniques I use give nearly instant results and provide new avenues of interests whilst on the research trail.

Price Guide

I have chosen to use the term Price Guide rather than Valuing, as value can be interpreted in many ways by many different collectors and dealers. Although the two are somewhat interlinked, pricing is the bottom line which a collector needs to know when considering a potential item for the collection.

Please bear in mind that this can only serve as a guide and cannot give a precise price for a particular piece, which is determined by a dealer or collector's individually perceived condition and uniqueness. Please take into consideration also, when using the Price Guide, that although correct at the time of writing in 2012, it is subject to change as time progresses, as is the case with all militaria. For example, in 2005 a Second World War RAF Officer's peak cap could sell for as little as £40 while now they tend to sell for around the £100, depending on where they are listed.

However, it is unwise and difficult to predict future prices, which can rely on various aspects such as the state of the economy or even the release of a new war film, which creates added interest in a collecting genre from new collectors or enthusiasts.

Specialised auction houses and militaria dealers tend to value their items higher than an internet auction, no doubt due to the fact that they attract more serious collectors. However we must also take into consideration that in general some dealers may only have had a limited experience of certain peak caps, or indeed caps in general, making what is unusual for them a rarity, but for a cap collector, a fairly common cap.

Furthermore, there seems to be some suspicion concerning the reliability of internet auctions, as they cannot always guarantee originality or even correct identification. This is perhaps not surprising as sellers tend not to be specialists in military collectables. However, it should also be mentioned that dealers are prone to errors or misidentification.

As internet auctions and other areas cannot give a true pricing guide, the amounts stated reflects the pricing used by dealers for a cap in the stated condition. Peak caps from certain branches or units, such as the Special Air Service or RAF & R/N Chaplains are quite scarce and would be priced accordingly. Due to the rarity of such items, I have chosen to restrict this price guide to caps that are more easily obtainable, but no less desirable.

Lastly it is worth highlighting that buying British peak caps from a non British based dealer might command a higher price for a certain piece, considering that piece would be less common in the dealer's country.

Condition

Before we move to the actual Pricing Guide I want to clarify the codes that I use for describing the condition of items in my collection. Regardless however of the condition, I find all items are displayable and can serve as original place holders or additions to the collection in their own right.

Near Mint Condition: The item is almost unworn with only minor marks or stress.

Above Average Condition: The item is in a very good state but has some obvious but minor damage, mothing/moth holes, or is missing a component.

Average Condition: The item is in a presentable state but has obvious damage/mothing or is missing a feature.

Below Average Condition: The item is quite grubby, damp or damaged. Significant fading to material or metal work.

Pricing Guide

As each dealer is different this pricing guide reflects caps that are in above average condition, unless otherwise stated.

British Army Undress Peak Cap	
Junior Officers	£35+
Junior Officers (new current issue)	£147+
Field Officers	£85+
Field Officers (new current issue)	£184+
Colonel/Brigadier	£125+
Colonel/Brigadier (post-war)	£120+
Colonel/Brigadier (new current issue)	£243+
General Officers	£425+
General Officers (post-war)	£220+
Scots Guards (or similar)	£350+
Scots Guards (or similar, new current issue)	£239+

British Army Service Cap	
Junior Officers	£40+
Junior Officers (new current issue)	£143+
Colonel/Brigadier	£125+
Colonel/Brigadier (post-war)	£65+
General Officers (post-war)	£100+
Metal badges	£10+

British Army Badges	
Field Marshall cap badge	£275+
Field Marshall cap badge, reproduction	£25+
General's cap badge	£85+
General's cap badge, reproduction	£25+
General's cap badge (post-war)	£65+
Brigadier/Colonel	£40+
Brigadier/Colonel, reproduction	£20+

Royal Navy

Junior Officers	£110+
Junior Officers (new current issue)	£140+
Lt. Cmdr	£75+
Lt. Cmdr (post-war)	£125+
Lt. Cmdr (new current issue)	£258+
Flag Officer (new current issue)	£290+
Merchant Marine Junior Officer	£65+
Royal Marine Junior Officer (new current issue)	£150+

Navy Badges (without band)

Royal Navy Officer cap badge	£35+
Royal Navy Officer "economy" cap badge	£35+
Royal Navy Officer (new current issue)	£60
Royal Navy Officer cap badge, reproduction	£20+
Royal Navy CPO P/O cap badge	£20+
Royal Navy CPO P/O "economy" cap badge	£25+
Merchant Navy cap badge	£10+

Royal Air Force

Junior Officers	£100+
Junior Officers (post-war)	£45+
Junior Officers (new current issue)	£149+
Group Captain	£285+
Group Captain (new current issue)	£375
Air rank	£485+
Air rank (post-war)	£240+
Air rank (new current issue)	£245+

RAF Badges (without band)

RAF WO cap badge	£20+
RAF Junior Officer cap badge	£35+
RAF Junior Officer (new current issue)	£60
RAF Junior Officer cap badge, reproduction	£20+
RAF Junior Officer gilt cap badge	£125+
RAF Junior Officers gilt beret badge	£20+
RAF Chaplains cap badge	£375+
RAF Chaplains (post-war) cap badge	£175+
RAF Air rank cap badge	£250+
RAF Air rank cap badge, reproduction	£25+
RAF Air rank (new current issue)	£80

CHAPTER ELEVEN

Care, Storage and Display

There are many techniques on how to store and display your collection, which can also depend on the amount of space that you have available. As collections are mostly a private thing, shared only perhaps with family and friends or over a forum/website, there is no official method and so as collectors we have to be creative and resourceful. However, participating in collecting forums, and contacting or visiting museums is a good way to gain information and ideas.

Care

Consisting mostly of cloth and leather, there are many issues that can affect a peak cap: gold-wire and metal tarnishing, moth holes and grazing, dampness, and surface mould. If a cap is or has not been properly stored then any one of these problems can occur.

Cloth dampness can be curable with a little warmth over a drying-out period, such as in an airing cupboard, however, the heat must not be too intense where it can affect the cap's main materials. Concerning leather dampness, this can take longer to resolve and you must be careful as too much heat can cause the leather to become brittle when dried out, in which case beeswax can be used for revitalisation, unless the leather has become too fragile. However rather than adding products or tampering too much with the cap, it is far better to adequately store and display it in the first place.

It is a sensitive issue for collectors as to whether or not an original item should be restored, preserved or merely left alone, especially if the process is irreversible. I do not believe in restoration, as having an untouched piece in my collection holds more interest and value, although for some poor examples which need a helping hand to stop further deterioration I can understand that some small amount of preservation is called for.

Regarding surface mould, this can easily be removed by using a slightly damp cloth to gently wipe it away. Unfortunately however, problems of mothing and metal tarnishing are irreversible, and as such cannot be treated. The best method is to create an environment where this can be prevented.

Storage/Archiving

The main point on storage must be the environment or room conditions. I store my caps at room temperature, away from dampness and cold. As space can often be limited to a collector, those items archived must be examined from time to time, to provide a fresh flow of air and wipe away any surface mould. It is also good to check their overall condition and the state of the metal work, to see if the storage needs to be altered.

Space allowing I use cardboard boxes inserted with moth pillows, balls or cards, or lavender bags if you have any available. The periodic examination also allows me to check the anti-moth devices and refresh them if needed.

For the cap, depending on its style, I place it resting on its top with the peak pointing into the air. I often add some padding in the area between the peak and the cap to support any potential peak movement, as well as in the lining to fill out the sweatband. If the cap is more of a saddle shape then I would rest the cap upright and support its body on a block or padding to even out the strain on the peak.

As with display, the aim is to make sure that the cap is not resting on its peak. Using a hat stretcher would also be a good solution for box storage, which would allow the cap to be fully supported.

When storing in a cupboard or wardrobe, not intended for "public" display, I employ a stacking method whereby the first cap is resting on its top, while another cap is positioned on top, the right way up but slightly offset so that the first cap's band is supporting that of the second. This takes the weight off the second cap's peaks. I also place anti-moth devices either in the caps or close by. While this method is not ideal as a long term solution it works fine as a temporary measure, since air can flow freely around the caps. It also allows the caps to be easily swapped around.

A cap showing surface mould resulting from bad storage. Usually gently wiping and drying out will restore the cap to its previous condition, unless the leather has been penetrated. From my experience, caps wrapped in bubble wrap minimise and even avoid such mould attacks, but make sure the cap is damp free before storing, otherwise this problem will persist, eventually staining the cloth permanently and destroying the leather. *Private Collection.*

Display

From my personal point of view, the method used for displaying a cap should preserve its original shape and support its peak. The cap must be supported as if it was being worn. When choosing a display option you have to consider the cap itself and the space you have available. Following are a list of options I have considered and used.

Display Heads

Display Heads come in a variety of styles and materials, such as wood, polystyrene and glass. Similar options are wooden hat blocks that are suitably shaped to give the peak and top support. Keep in mind that you will need to consider the height space that you have available.

The photographed display has a base diameter of 18cm and a height of 28cm. I particularly like the weathered facial features on this example, which complement nicely to a cap it is displaying.

The disadvantages of a display head is that as they are mass-produced and so it is not always possible to find a size that fits exactly to your cap. This can result in the cap gradually loosing shape, over a period of time, from lack of support around its band. Some smaller sized caps literally perch onto the top of the head which is not such an issue for a photographing session or a short term display.

Paper, Cloth & Cushions

Rolled up paper, T-shirts or small cushions can support the cap's shape although might not provide enough strength to relieve stress from the peak. Alternatively, resting the cap on a cushion can allow the cushion to mould around the cap. However these options should only be considered when the cap is displayed for short periods of time, as I personally feel that the peak is not adequately supported.

Display heads can be a good option for exhibits and displays. They exist in various materials and sizes. I particularly like this example because of its facial features, as well as the fact that the polystyrene is softer on my caps than a glass example. *Private Collection.*

Example of permanent damage caused to a cap's top by an inappropriate display technique. *Private Collection.*

Stands

While peak caps displayed on stands, wooden or otherwise, eliminate the strain from the peak, some such stands have a small flat or convex surface support area which can, over time, develop non-reversible damage. I do not favour this option. However if the stand has a convex support area that fully supports the top as well as the sweatband area, then such a stand should be considered.

Artillery Shells and Tubes

Do not rest your caps over old artillery shells or tubes. While this may look good in a photograph it will not do your cap any favours in the long term, as again this can cause non-reversible damage and/or distortion to the cap's top.

Hat Stretchers and Specialised Displays

Wooden hat stretchers are a popular solution with collectors, as the blocks can be adjusted to fit the cap's size. However be aware that over tightening can cause damage by unnecessary strain. Depending on the height of the stretcher itself, the cap can be positioned so that the peak is off the ground and thus supported. On some stretcher examples the cap's top is not supported and left to hang naturally, which might be a disadvantage in the long run, unless cushioned.

The wooden cap display used throughout this book was crafted by the specialist Skipper Greenwade, and as can be seen from the photographs, this is not only an attractive solution using honest neutral looking materials, but provides the best support for the cap.

The top section of the Greenwade display stand inserted into an Army Forage cap. It's size can be adjusted to fit the cap's sweatband, replicating the head of the wearer and thus maintaining the cap's original shape. *Private Collection.*

A headgear display from Skipper Greenwade. This versatile stand is perfect for peak caps, as it allows the peak to remain off the ground whilst at the same time providing support to the cap's body. Extra padding can be inserted to stop the top from sagging. *Private Collection.*

GLOSSARY

Below are a list of terms used in this book, as well as some added abbreviations that are relevant to this topic and might prove helpful.

ADC: Army Dental Corps.
AEC: Army Educational Corps.
Astral crown: Used in aviation, similar in appearance to the Merchant Navy crown.
Bi-metal: White metal and gilt used for metal cap badges.
Blackhorn buttons: Made from processed horn and formed into a button shape.
Bronze: Copper and tin alloy metal used for dress cap badges
CPO: Royal Navy rank of Chief Petty Officer.
DL: Deputy Lieutenant.
EiiR: Royal Cypher of Queen Elizabeth II. Reigned from 1952 onwards.
EviiiR: Royal Cypher of King Edward VIII. Reigned from January to December 1936.
Forage cap: Undress or Dress cap, generally known post-war as the No.1 Dress cap.
Gilt: Gold plated gilded metal used for Service cap badges.
Gold wire: Also known as bullion thread. Coiled gold plated wire used on embroidered cap badges.
GvR: Royal Cypher of King George V. Reigned from 1910 to 1936.
GviR: Royal Cypher of King George VI. Reigned from 1936 to 1952.
Hessian: Also known as Burlap. Thickly woven material produced from the Jute plant, mostly used as stiffeners in cap construction.
HMCE: HM Customs & Excise.
Inter-war: The period between 1919-1939.
KC/GR crown/Imperial Crown: The Tudor crown or King's crown which was used from 1901 to 1953 on cap badges and buttons, denoting the authority of the Monarch.
LDV: Local Defence Volunteers (or from July 1940, known as the Home Guard).
Lt.Cmdr: Royal Navy rank of Lieutenant Commander.
Lug & pin: Cap badge attachment consisting of two loops that are welded to the badge, through which a separate "hairpin"is inserted. (Pin & Loop attachment).
MN: Merchant Navy.
NSN: NATO Stock Numbers. A standardised system for cataloguing military equipment, including uniform items, used primarily by members of the North Atlantic Treaty Organization (NATO).
Oak-leaf: Embroidered peak decoration used on high ranking Officer's peak caps, displaying a half wreath of oak leaves. Often referred to as "scrambled eggs."
Oilcloth: A material consisting of linseed oil covered canvas, used mostly as backing material or peak rims.
Oilskin: A similar material to oilcloth but usually thinner and more transparent, used mostly for sweat protectors.
Patent leather: Treated leather creating a black glossy varnished finish which was used for cap peaks, rims and chinstraps up until the 1960s.
Plasticised leather: leather coated in black plastic.
P/O: Royal Navy rank of Petty Officer.
Post-war: The period mainly from 1953 to current.
Pre-war: The period before 1939, mainly the inter-war years.
QC/ERII crown/Coronation Crown: The St Edward's (or Queen's crown) used from 1953 to the present day, on cap badges and buttons, denoting the authority of the reigning Monarch.
RAAF: Royal Australian Air Force.
RAF: The Royal Air Force.
RAFVR: Royal Air Force Volunteer Reserve.
RAN: The Royal Australian Navy.
RAMC: Royal Army Medical Corps.
RAOC: Royal Army Ordnance Corps.
RAPC: Royal Army Pay Corps.
RAVC: Royal Army Veterinary Corps.
RCAF: The Royal Canadian Air Force.
REME: The Royal Electrical and Mechanical Engineers.
RFA: Royal Fleet Auxiliary.
RM: Royal Marines.
R/N: The Royal Navy.
RND: The Royal Naval Division. Formed in 1914 from Royal Marines and reserve RN Officers and men, the RND served throughout the First World War.
RNR: Royal Naval Reserve.
RNVR: Royal Naval Volunteer Reserve.
RNZAF: The Royal New Zealand Air Force.
Royal Crest: Lion surmounting the Monarch's crown motif.
Royal Cypher: The Monarch's monogram surmounted by their crown.
SAAF: South African Air Force.
Sealed Patterns: An example of a uniform accoutrement or insignia that provides a reference pattern for Outfitters and manufacturers. The garment or item is usually attached to a label detailing the sealed date, pattern number and item description, among other things. A metal or wax seal bearing the motif of the inspectorate is usually fixed to the label ribbon. Sealed Patterns were kept at the Admiralty, Air Ministry and War Office, while some copies were also kept by each regiment.
Service cap: A cap used for general service wear, usually made of a lower quality material than the Dress cap.
Silver: Cap badges made from Sterling silver.
Skiver: Thin textured leather used mostly on peak undersides (often green in colour).
Split-pins: Cap badge attachment consisting of two blades that are bent into position after the badge has been fitted to the cap. Also used on air vent backings.
Stay-bright (or **Staybrite**): Cap badge or buttons made from anodised aluminium.
Vinyl: PVC plastic material used mostly for chinstraps and peaks.
W/O: Rank of Warrant Officer.
WWII: The Second World War or World War II.

BIBLIOGRAPHY

The bibliography has been presented in order of chapter to allow easier reference for further reading.

Books and Documentation

Epigraph

Hector Powe. Naval, Military, R.A.F and Civil Tailors, in: *The Royal Navy Officer's Pocket-Book, 1944.* Conway, 2007."Remember, the Cap is the most important. It can make or mar your appearance."

Chapter 1: Introduction & History

J.D. & Co. Ltd. in: *Sealed Pattern label* 1940, *"to guide make and shape."*

Brian Lavery, *In Which They Served*, Conway, 2008.

David Nash, *The Prussian Army 1808-1815*, Almark Publishing, 1972.

H.M.S.O., *Dress Regulations for the Army*, London, 1859.

H.M.S.O., *Dress Regulations for the Army*, London, 1864.

H.M.S.O., *Uniform Regulations for Officers, Petty Officers, and Seaman of the Fleet, London*, 1879.

H.M.S.O., *Dress Regulations for the Officers of the Army*, London, 1904.

H.M.S.O., *Dress Regulations for the Officers of the Army*, London, 1934. 1938. Reproduced by The Naval & Military Press Ltd.

National Maritime Museum, *The Dress of Naval Officers*, H.M.S.O., 1966.

Stuart Bates, *British Army Forage Caps 1840s-1890s*, Document. May 28th 2012.

Frédéric Coune, *Le Casque Français 1915-1945*, Uniformes – Hors-Série n°28, 3e trimestre 2011.

Chapter 3, 4: British Army

Brian L Davis, *British Army Uniforms & Insignia of World War Two*, Arms & Armour, 1992.

Adjutant-General's Office, *Regulations for the dress of General, Staff, and Regimental Officers of the Army, London*, 1857.

H.M.S.O., *Dress Regulations for the Officers of the Army*, London, 1904.

H.M.S.O., *Dress Regulations for the Officers of the Army*, London, 1934. 1938. Reproduced by The Naval & Military Press Ltd.

Edited by E.C. Talbot-Booth Paymr. Lt.Cmdr. R.N.R. *Rank and Badges in the Navy, Army, R.A.F and Auxiliaries,* George Philip & Son, Ltd, London, 1941.

Chapter 5: The Royal Air Force

H.M.S.O, *Dress Regulations for Officers of the Royal Air Force*, 1939.

H.M.S.O., *Dress regulations for the Air Training Corps*, 1944.

Carl. A. Christie, *Ocean Bridge The History of RAF Ferry Command*, University of Toronto Press, 1997.

Humphrey Wynn, *Forged in War, A History of Royal Air Force Transport Command 1943-1967,* H.M.S.O, London 1996.

Edited by E.C. Talbot-Booth Paymr. Lt.Cmdr. R.N.R. *Rank and Badges in the Navy, Army, R.A.F and Auxiliaries,* George Philip & Son, Ltd., London, 1941.

Chapter 6: The Royal Navy

H.M.S.O., *Uniform Regulations for Officers of the Fleet*, London, 1937.

National Maritime Museum, *The Dress of Naval Officers*, H.M.S.O., 1966.

Ian Summer, *The Royal Navy 1939-1945,* Osprey Publishing, 2001.

Edited by E.C. Talbot-Booth Paymr. Lt.Cmdr. R.N.R. *Rank and Badges in the Navy, Army, R.A.F and Auxiliaries,* George Philip & Son, Ltd, London, 1941.

Complied and introduced by Brian Lavery, *The Royal Navy Officer's Pocket-Book, 1944.* Conway, 2007.

Chapter 7: Commonwealth Peak Caps

J.O. Patenaude. I.S.O., *Dress Regulations for the Royal Canadian Air Force 1925 (1939)*, 1939.

Compiled by George P. Quigley, An RCAF 80th Anniversary Project of The Francis Grainger Quigley Memorial Collection. Compilation ©1991, 2006.

Richard Williams, *These are Facts - the Autobiography of Air Marshal Sir Richard Williams KBE CB DSO*, Australian War Memorial, 1977.

Chapter 8: Post-war Peak Caps & Dating a Peak Cap

Ministry of Defence, *Rifles Headdress Suppliers for Officers and WO1*, 2010.

Ministry of Defence, *Dress Regulations for Royal Logistics Corp*, 2010.

Ministry of Defence, *Dress Regulations for The Mercian Regiment*, 2009.

The Regimental Charity of the Duke of Lancaster's Regiment, *The Regimental Handbook of the Duke of Lancaster's Regiment*, Preston, 2009.

Ministry of Defence, *Uniform Dress and Appearance Regulations for the Royal Air Force, Princess Mary's Royal Air Force Nursing Service Auxiliary and Reserve Forces*, 2004.

National Maritime Museum, *The Dress of Naval Officers*, H.M.S.O., 1966.

Complied and introduced by Brian Lavery, *The Royal Navy Officer's Pocket-Book, 1944.* Conway, 2007.

Stuart Bates, *British Army Forage Caps 1840s-1890s*, Document. May 28th 2012.

Chapter 9: Outfitters

Elizabeth Hughes, Marion Lester, *The Big Book of Buttons*, New Leaf Publishers, 1991.

Blue Plaque, *Isaac Simpson 1800-1859 and Stephen Simpson 1832-1891.* Preston & South Ribble Civic Trust.

Glossary
Complied by Joyce M. Hawkins, *Oxford Paperback Dictionary, 3rd Edition,* Oxford University Press, 1988.

Electronic Resources

Chapter 1: Introduction & History
Oxford University Press, *Definition of shako*, viewed November 10 2012, http://oxforddictionaries.com/definition/english/shako?q=shako

Chapter 4: British Army
St George's Chapel Windsor Castle, *About the College, Who's Who, The Military Knights of Windsor*, viewed November 10 2012, http://www.stgeorges-windsor.org/about-st-georges/whos-who/military-knights.html

Chapter 6: The Royal Navy
The Imperial War Museum, *Badge, headdress, British, cap tally, sealed pattern, Royal Navy*, viewed April 15 2012, http://www.iwm.org.uk/collections/item/object/30063791
The Royal Marines Museum, *Marines Uniform*, viewed April 15 2012, http://www.royalmarinesmuseum.co.uk/item/researching-family-and-royal-marine-history/marines-unforms
Royal Navy, *Royal Fleet Auxiliary*, viewed April 15 2012, http://www.royalnavy.mod.uk/The-Fleet/Royal-Fleet-Auxiliary
Royal Fleet Auxiliary, *Maritime Trades Unions, ROYAL FLEET AUXILIARY Flexible Global Reach - Future Manning Strategy*, June 14 2006, viewed April 15 2012, http://www.rmt.org.uk/Shared_ASP_Files/UploadedFiles/D4C19F16-D36C-4350-B5F2-ECA555CAD85B_rfasubmission.pdf
HM Waterguard, *What is the Waterguard?*, viewed April 15 2012, http://www.hm-waterguard.org.uk/Help%20&%20FAQs.htm#WHAT WAS THE WATERGUARD?
HM Waterguard, *The Waterguard Uniform*, viewed April 15 2012, http://www.hm-waterguard.org.uk/Uniform.htm#CAPS_WATERGUARD
HM Waterguard, *The History of The Waterguard*, viewed April 15 2012,
http://www.hm-waterguard.org.uk/History.htm
The Imperial War Museum, ON BOARD HMS RODNEY. SEPTEMBER 1940, ROMAN CATHOLIC CHAPLAINS ARE NOT CARRIED IN ALL SHIPS, viewed November 10 2012, http://www.iwm.org.uk/collections/item/object/205185091

Chapter 8: Post-war Peak Caps & Dating a Peak Cap
The REME Museum of Technology, *REME Old Style Cap Badge,* viewed May 4 2012, http://www.rememuseum.org.uk/uniforms.aspx?shopid=2
The Royal Signals Museum, *The original style of cap badge,* viewed May 4 2012, http://www.royalsignalsmuseum.co.uk/WebSite/index.php/royal-signals-history/2011-10-26-23-11-03/cap-badge-history
The DLI Museum, *Forage Cap, 68 LI,* viewed May 17 2012, http://ww2.durham.gov.uk/dlimuseum/pgObjects.aspx?&ID=5675&CODE=10&CATDESC=Hats&WEB=MAIN&SEARCH=
THE NATO CODIFICATION SYSTEM:, *1.6.5. NATO STOCK NUMBER – NSN,* viewed June 30 2012, http://www.nato.int/structur/ac/135/ncs_guide/english/e_1-6-5.htm
The U.S. Government Cataloging and National Stock Number System, *NSNs and Cataloging History*, viewed June 30 2012, http://www.helpdesk365.org/cataloging.htm
NSN (NATO Stock Number) structure, *NATO Stock Number (NSN) Structure,* viewed June 30 2012, http://www.leafieldlogistics.co.uk/36/NSN_NATO_Stock_Number_structure/
The Imperial War Museum, *badge, headdress, British, The Worcestershire Regiment, other ranks*, viewed July 6 2012, http://www.iwm.org.uk/collections/item/object/30076238

Chapter 9: Outfitters
Toye & Co., *History 1950 to Present*, viewed July 9 2012, http://www.toye.com/about-us/history-1950-present
Gieves & Hawkes, *James Gieve*, viewed November 14 2012, http://discover.gievesandhawkes.com/discover-gieves-and-hawkes-tailoring/history/james-gieve

Chapter 10: Researching and Price Guide
Herbert Johnson, *Uniform Headwear,* viewed November 10 2012, http://www.herbert-johnson.co.uk/products2.html
Gieves & Hawkes Military, *Headwear,* viewed 27 August 2012, http://www.gievesandhawkesmilitary.com/acatalog/headwear.html

Chapter 11: Care, Storage and Display
Skipper Greenwade, *Headgear Displays,* viewed 27 August 2012, http://www.skippergreenwade.com/Headgear%20Displays.htm

Terms
The Royal Naval Museum, Portsmouth, *The Royal Naval Division,* viewed November 10 2012, http://www.royalnavalmuseum.org/info_sheets_RND.htm
Oxford University Press, *Oxford Dictionaries*, viewed November 10 2012, http://oxforddictionaries.com/
The Royal Anglian & Royal Lincolnshire Regimental Association, *Abbreviations,* viewed November 10 2012, http://www.thelincolnshireregiment.org/abbreviations.shtml#R